Lillian Too's
Easy-to-use
Feng Shui

This book is dedicated to my very precious lama,
the Venerable Lama Zopa Rinpoche

for my daughter
Jennifer Too and for my husband Too Wan Jin

and for the ultimate happiness
of every living being

Lillian Too's Easy-to-use Feng Shui

168 ways to success

COLLINS & BROWN

First published in June 1998 as Lillian Too's Personalised Feng Shui Tips
by Konsep Books, Malaysia

First published in Great Britain in 1999
by Collins & Brown Limited
London House
Great Eastern Wharf
Parkgate Road
London SW11 4NQ

Distributed in the United States and Canada by Sterling Publishing Co,
387 Park Avenue South, New York, NY 10016, USA

3 5 7 9 8 6 4 2
British Library Cataloguing-in-Publication Data:
A catalogue record for this title is
available from the British Library.

ISBN 185585 740 5 (hardback)
ISBN 185585 690 5 (paperback)

Edited and designed by
Collins & Brown Limited

Editor: Susan Martineau
Consultant editor: Mary Lambert
Graphic design: Jerry Goldie
Picture researcher: Gabrielle Allen
Artworks: Kate Simunek

Reproduction by Global Colour, Malaysia
Printed by New Interlitho, Italy

You can contact Lillian Too on the internet at her web sites:
www.worldoffengshui.com and www.lillian-too.com

Contents

Chapter three
Feng Shui In Your Office

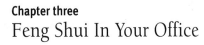

Chapter four
Feng Shui To Boost Your Career

Chapter five
Feng Shui For Better Wealth Luck

Chapter six
Feng Shui For Different Rooms In The House

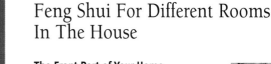

Lunar Calendar Conversion 1924–1995

This is the Lunar Calendar that you will need to use to work out your personal KUA number, which is referred to in Tip 1 and many times throughout the book.

YEAR	Lunar Year starts in	YEAR	Lunar Year starts in
1924	Feb 5th	1959	Feb 8th
1925	Jan 24th	1960	Jan 28th
1926	Feb 13th	1961	Feb 15th
1927	Feb 2nd	1962	Feb 5th
1928	Jan 23rd	1963	Jan 25th
1929	Feb 10th	1964	Feb 13th
1930	Jan 30th	1965	Feb 2nd
1931	Feb 17th	1966	Jan 21st
1932	Feb 6th	1967	Feb 9th
1933	Jan 26th	1968	Jan 30th
1934	Feb 14th	1969	Feb 17th
1935	Feb 4th	1970	Feb 6th
1936	Jan 24th	1971	Jan 27th
1937	Feb 11th	1972	Feb 15th
1938	Jan 31st	1973	Feb 3rd
1939	Feb 19th	1974	Jan 23rd
1940	Feb 8th	1975	Feb 11th
1941	Jan 27th	1976	Jan 31st
1942	Feb 15th	1977	Feb 18th
1943	Feb 5th	1978	Feb 7th
1944	Jan 25th	1979	Jan 28th
1945	Feb 13th	1980	Feb 16th
1946	Feb 2nd	1981	Feb 5th
1947	Jan 22nd	1982	Jan 25th
1948	Feb 10th	1983	Feb 13th
1949	Jan 29th	1984	Feb 2nd
1950	Feb 17th	1985	Feb 20th
1951	Feb 6th	1986	Feb 9th
1952	Jan 27th	1987	Jan 29th
1953	Feb 14th	1988	Feb 17th
1954	Feb 3rd	1989	Feb 6th
1955	Jan 24th	1990	Jan 27th
1956	Feb 12th	1991	Feb 15th
1957	Jan 31st	1992	Feb 4th
1958	Feb 18th	1993	Jan 23rd
		1994	Feb 10th
		1995	Jan 31st

A personal wish from Lillian Too

It has been five years since I wrote my first feng shui book to introduce this magnificent practice to the world and to preserve a valuable heritage and tradition of the Chinese people. I certainly did not realize then that feng shui would become so popular in so many countries, but this is because it really does improve lives and luck at very little cost and effort!

Many wonderful people are responsible for this revival of interest in feng shui – old masters, traditional practitioners and new-age enthusiasts. Many writers have played valuable roles in spreading the vogue of feng shui, by unselfishly sharing their knowledge and promoting this ancient practice – in the process, enhancing and improving the lives of many people. I salute especially the pioneer writers who, many years ago share their fledgling discovery of feng shui with the English speaking world. Writers like Derek Walters, Stephen Skinner, Sarah Rossbach, Kwok Man Ho, Evelyn Lip and Raymond Lo to name but a few. Today there are many engaged in disseminating what they have learnt from localized masters and old practitioners. Some of course do it better than others, and some are more genuinely authentic than others, but all play a valuable role in increasing awareness of this wonderful practice.

Basic feng shui is easy to learn. But it is a subject that has great breadth of formulas and incredible depth of analysis and practice. For me personally, the continuous availability of more in-depth information astounds me. I am also guided in my writing by the numerous letters and e-mails I get. These communications from my readers help me improve explanations of all the feng shui recommendations I offer.

People's personal Kua numbers and their auspicious directions are referred to several times in the book so I have included a lunar calendar on the previous page so that you can easily work out your own number.

This book has been written in response to the growing demand for easy-to-use feng shui tips that can be used in daily living. In putting together this book I have called on my store of old books and notes on feng shui. I loved writing this book, and I genuinely hope something inside this book brings every reader the good fortune they each want.

ENRICHING YOUR PERSONAL SPACE

1

Determine Your Auspicious Corners

The best way to start in the practice of personal feng shui is first to determine the four corners of your living space that are most auspicious for you. These will be your 'lucky spots' in any room, office or apartment you occupy. Sitting, sleeping or working in any of these four specific locations will generally bring you good luck, and protect you from bad luck. The formula used for identifying these lucky locations is part of what is called Compass School feng shui.

Your KUA Number

To determine your auspicious directions you will need to calculate your KUA number. If you were born between 1 January and 20 February you will need to check the date on which the lunar New Year occurred in your year of birth (see page 8). If you were born before the New Year, you must subtract one from your year of birth before proceeding to make the calculation of the KUA number, for example, if you were born on the 7 February 1964 then you should count your year of birth as 1963. This is because in that year the lunar New Year occurred on the 13 February.

Once you have ascertained your correct lunar year of birth, you can proceed to calculate your KUA number using this simple formula. Take the last two digits of your year of birth and add the numbers. Keep adding until it is reduced to a single number, for example, if your year of birth is 1968, adding 6+8 will equal 14, then add 1+4 which equals 5. Then if you are male you should deduct your last number from 10, so 10-5=5 so your KUA number is 5. If you are female you should add 5 to your last number, so 5+5=10 and then 1+0=1 so the KUA number is 1 for a female born in 1968 and 5 for a male born in 1968.

With your KUA number check the table here to determine your auspicious directions and also to work out if you are a WEST person or an EAST person.

Auspicious Corners & Locations

YOUR KUA NUMBER	YOUR AUSPICIOUS CORNERS & LOCATIONS IN DESCENDING ORDER OF LUCK	ARE YOU AN EAST OR WEST GROUP PERSON?
1	South-east, East, South, North	East
2	North-east, West, North-west, South-west	West
3	South, North, South-east, East	East
4	North, South, East, South-east	East
5	MEN: North-east, West, North-west, South-west	
	WOMEN: South-west, North-west, West, North-east	West
6	West, North-east, South-west, North-west	West
7	North-west, South-west, North-east, West	West
8	South-west, North-west, West, North-east	West
9	East, South-east, North, South	East

Note that West group corners are inauspicious for East group people and vice versa.

Find Your Good Fortune Directions

2

Compass School feng shui is based on personal birth dates and gender. The compass points that indicate auspicious locations also indicate the best directions. Thus, when determining your sitting and sleeping directions, you must also know what your personal best directions are. Refer to the table below and memorize the directions that are auspicious for you. Then try, as far as possible, always to sit directly facing your most auspicious direction. In instances where this is physically not possible, you should then try to use at least one of your other three good directions. They may not be your best ones but it is infinitely better to sit facing an acceptable direction than to sit facing one

Auspicious & Inauspicious Directions

Your KUA number	1	2	3	4	5	6	7	8	9
AUSPICIOUS DIRECTIONS									
Your sheng chi or your success direction	SE	NE	S	N	NE SW	W	NW	SW	E
Your tien yi or health direction	E	W	N	S	W NW	NE	SW	NW	SE
Your nien yen or romance direction	S	NW	SE	E	NW W	SW	NE	W	N
Your fu wei or personal development direction	N	SW	E	SE	SW NE	NW	W	NE	S
INAUSPICIOUS DIRECTIONS									
Your ho hai or unlucky direction	W	E	SW	NW	E S	SE	N	S	NE
Your wu kwei or five ghosts direction	NE	SE	NW	SW	SE N	E	S	N	W
Your lui sha or six killings direction	NW	S	NE	W	S E	N	SE	E	SW
Your chueh ming or total loss direction	SW	N	W	NE	N SE	S	E	SE	NW

that is inauspicious and spells total loss for you! The formula describes the types of good and bad luck of all the eight directions of the compass. 'Five ghosts' means five types of bad luck in the form of obstacles to success and 'six killings' represent extreme bad luck such as illnesses, accidents or betrayals. The directions are based on individual KUA numbers (see Tip 1) and are listed in the table above. For KUA number 5, the top directions are for men and those below for women.

Buy yourself a good, orienteering, oil-filled compass so that you can work out your most auspicious directions wherever you are.

3

Be Aware of the Energies in Your Space

How can you tell if you are suffering from bad feng shui? I have often been asked this question, and my advice has been for people to get into the habit of developing awareness of their surroundings. Be sensitive to the occurrence of things going wrong, especially when there seems to be a pattern and a frequency that seems to suggest a spate of bad luck. Shakespeare said, 'troubles come not in ones and twos but in battalions'. He could have been describing the effect of bad feng shui. This is because bad luck that is caused by bad feng shui happens almost continuously.

The effect of unbalanced energies, or of being hit by 'killing breath', often causes things to go wrong with no respite. Your environment and the physical structures that occupy your personal space emanate many different kinds of energies all the time. These energies can be gross or subtle, and they are either benevolent or treacherous. In other words they can bring good luck or misfortune. So you should try to tune into the energies that surround your personal space. You do not need to become obsessed with feng shui, but you will benefit enormously if you develop sensitivity to how these energies affect your living space. The best times to 'check' the feng shui of your personal space are when you have just moved into a new home or office; and during the changeover of years and decades, e.g. during the lunar new year.

Energy Flow

Consciously monitor subtle changes in the space and time dimensions of your home. Feng shui is all about changing the energies of space and time. So, observe the flow as you walk through your space. If your flow is meandering and leisurely, the energies will be more auspicious than if the flow is straight and fast. Too many nooks and corners will cause obstacles to your flow, and are thus bad news. Your life will not be smooth. Obstacles frequently prevent you from attaining your goals. When your flow keeps coming to a stop, the same effect occurs. Be sensitive to how you have to move within your space by the way you have placed your furniture, or by the layout of your rooms and how you have placed your furniture within them.

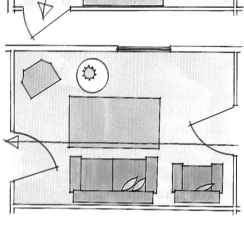

In this room the energy flow is good as it can meander around the furniture and out of the second door.

Here, the flow of energy is bad as the energy rushes straight in through one door and out of the other.

Identify Inauspicious Structures Around You

I once followed the progress of a huge mansion being built in my neighbourhood. The house was enormous, and the people building it were obviously wealthy. Surely they must have consulted a feng shui master I thought, since the main front door had been oriented awkwardly, probably to tap the best direction for the residents. Sadly, the house was destined for bad luck because the front door opened directly on to a decorative column. This pillar stood smack in the middle of the foyer facing the grand entrance into the home. Barely three months after they occupied the completed home, the father of the family had a heart attack, and the family business collapsed.

So, always take note of every structure that occupies your space, and try to nullify their bad feng shui effects by either blocking them from view with plants or screens or nullifying their effects with lights.

Pillars

Structural square pillars that block doors are always bad. Wrap them with mirrors or, better still, use a creeper plant to block off the sharp edges. Round pillars are not as harmful but when they directly confront your main door, they can be quite deadly. Place screens between them and the main door.

Spiral Staircases

These are really quite inauspicious structures to have around and, if placed in the centre of the home, they can spell disaster. The spaces in between the steps cause 'money' to drain away, and the circular corkscrew effect of the

Above Open spiral staircases are not good to have in the home as they can cause you to lose money, but a solid, curving staircase is fine provided it does not face the front door.

shape symbolizes great damage being done to the home.

Screens

Decorative room dividers should never stand as shown below as they create deadly poison arrows of hostile energy. Place them straight, either hanging suspended from the ceiling or or on the ground. Screens can make excellent feng shui cures, especially in slowing down inauspicious fast-moving energy.

Left Decorative screens can be good for shielding bad elements in a room, but make sure that you stand the screen straight and not as shown here, because you are creating poison arrows.

ENRICHING YOUR PERSONAL SPACE

5

Counter 'Arrows' That Hit Your Main Door

No house with a main door that is hit by the 'killing energy' of secret poison arrows can enjoy good feng shui. No matter how 'correct' the directions and orientations, the colour scheme and all other things, a single deadly poison arrow – anything that is pointed, sharp, straight and hostile – can destroy any carefully crafted feng shui features and orientations. So it is absolutely vital for the feng shui practitioner to identify anything in the immediate environment, inside and outside the home, which can symbolize this poison arrow.

Exterior poison arrows are usually more deadly and more difficult to cope with. Usually there is little one can do about the sharp edges of a neighbouring straight road that seems to be aimed directly at one's main front door. The best method of coping with such a dangerous structure is to re-orientate the door if at all possible. Change the door direction completely or use another door and close up the afflicted one. Hanging an eight-sided Pa Kua mirror or a five-rod windchime to confront the structure can help to some extent, but the most effective method is really to change the placement and location of the main door.

The Pa Kua

The eight-sided Pa Kua symbol hung above the front door is a very powerful feng shui antidote. This Pa Kua is known as the yin Pa Ku, and its power comes from its arranged sequence of tri-grams placed on each of the eight sides. This special yin arrangement is often referred to as the Early Heaven Arrangement. The mirror in the centre can be convex or concave. Both versions work. Always hang the Pa Kua outside the home. Never hang it inside the home or the office. It has the power to cause havoc and destroy all your good feng shui indoors. The Pa Kua mirror is used outside only and always facing away from the house!

Bad Shar

If you have a road coming straight towards your home and cannot move your door, you can trying hanging a Pa Kua mirror above the door to deflect the bad shar. The Pa Kua is a very powerful symbol. In view of this, please use it with care. Don't have it facing towards your neighbours. If you can, always use other cures where possible.

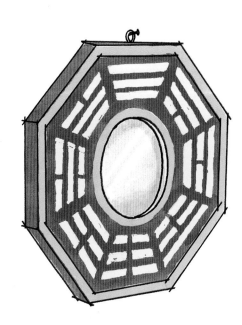

Sleep With Your Head Positioned Correctly

6

If you have a choice of bedrooms, select the one that is located in your most auspicious location. This means it should be the bedroom in the corner of the building corresponding to your best direction, i.e. your sheng chi direction (see Tip 2).

If it is not possible for you to have a 'sheng chi' bedroom, try at least to get a bedroom in the part of the building that corresponds to one of your other good directions. If this, too, is not possible there is no need to fret. It is impossible for anyone to get everything perfect.

What you must have, however, is a bed that is positioned in such a way that your head is pointed towards one of your best directions. It is essential that, while you sleep, excellent auspicious energy is flowing into you from your sheng chi direction. This is a powerful method of enjoying really excellent feng shui. If you really cannot tap your sheng chi sleeping direction, again try to tap one of your other auspicious directions.

So, if you have a choice, always select what I call your sheng chi bedroom for success in your career or business. If your personal sheng chi direction is North then go for the bedroom that is placed in the North corner of your house. If this is not possible then you should try very hard to sleep with your head pointed to the North or, at the least, one of the other three of your auspicious directions. Of course, it is much easier to control your sleeping direction since this depends on the simple act of moving your bed until your head is pointed towards the direction that you want.

Try to place your bed so that you can sleep with your head pointing towards your auspicious direction. But, in doing this, do not let your feet point directly at the door. Also check that you are not affected by other bad feng shui features.

Bed Direction

In making the decision on your bed direction, you must also make very sure that:

- you are not sleeping directly under a beam
- you are not being 'hit' by the edge of a protruding corner
- you do not have your feet directly pointed to the door
- you do not have your head or toes pointed to a toilet
- you do not have the bed headboard directly under a window.

7

Sit In Your Best Feng Shui Position

When you are in a business meeting, try to sit in one of your auspicious directions. If it is difficult to get right, don't forget you can always swivel your body to a better position.

Where we sit and the direction we face while sitting create good or bad feng shui depending on our personal KUA numbers (see Tip 1). Thus where we sit at work, and what direction we face while negotiating, giving a presentation, or making a speech, affects our luck often to a significant extent. In the same way, how our chairs are positioned when we eat, work or simply socialize, can all have feng shui implications.

It is possible consciously to improve our luck merely by focusing on our sitting arrangements. So you should make certain your office table and chair are positioned to capture your most auspicious directions and placement and, when you sit at home, do the same thing.

Using Compasses

In personalized feng shui I always recommend everyone I meet to memorize their individual auspicious directions and carry a compass around with them so that there is never a time when one does not sit facing at least one of the four good directions.

Usually, irrespective of which direction our chair is pointed to, it is possible to 'swivel' your body to capture at least one of your four good directions. So, when you are interviewing, taking an exam, or at a meeting that is not held in your place of work or study, use this method to ensure that you are at least facing one of your good directions.

Direct Action
● When out on an important dinner date, and the occasion is romantic, sit facing your nien yen direction. It will enhance good feelings.
● When taking an exam sit facing your fu wei direction– it will give you the edge.
● When at an interview or important meeting sit facing your sheng chi direction. It will increase your chances of success.

Good Eating Feng Shui Brings Good Luck

8

One of the most wonderful features to have in your home is a large mirror, perhaps a wall mirror, in your dining room. This brings the best kind of eating feng shui. It symbolically doubles the food on the table. Placing a mirror in the North energizes the essence of protection for the household's livelihood, assuring the family of continued well-being. It does not guarantee wealth and riches but ensures the family will never lack for food.

Please note, however, that placing a mirror next to your stove is simply not the same thing and you will be creating very dangerous feng shui. It leads to severe physical danger, and you could well break a leg or an arm if you do this. Mirrors in the dining room enhance your fortunes. Mirrors in the kitchen bring grave danger into your life.

Another wonderful tip to magnify eating feng shui is to hang a picture of delicious-looking ripe fruit in the dining room. Placing a bowl of fruit on the dining table is also excellent. This creates beautiful energy that symbolizes the availability of food in the home. In the same way always make certain your refrigerator is well stocked and that you never run out of basic foodstuffs.

Placing bowls of fruit on the dining table is a good way of showing that food is always available in the home. Hanging a mirror opposite the table will create the effect of doubling the food.

Take Care of Your 'Rice Bowl'

9

In China the rice bowl symbolizes a family's livelihood, and Chinese families of the old tradition go to great lengths to observe certain 'rules' with respect to the rice bowl. These rules were handed down by word of mouth from members of the older generation, often from grandmothers and, as such, are often dismissed as superstition by the modern generation. In recent years, however, interest in feng shui as a way of living harmoniously with the energies of one's personal space has encouraged a more accepting attitude towards traditional advice. Many of today's Western-educated Chinese, in rediscovering their roots are practising feng shui by carefully taking care of the family rice bowl.

10 Understanding the Four Pillars in Feng Shui

The Four Pillars of destiny is one of the main methods used in Chinese fortune-telling. The four pillars are your year, month, day and hour of birth. From this information Chinese fortune tellers calculate what are referred to as the Eight Characters. These eight characters are the elements of feng shui – wood, water, earth, fire and metal – with a yin or yang aspect. Each of your 'pillars' corresponds to two elements which are given the names 'heavenly stem' and 'earthly branch'. The method of feng shui that uses the four pillars analyses each individual's eight elements and from there determines the elements that are deemed to be 'missing' from the birth chart. Enhancing the missing elements in the personal space is believed to then strengthen the individual's feng shui.

The calculation of one's personal four pillars and eight character chart is a very complicated process and does not lend itself easily to accuracy without a great deal of experience. In Hong Kong, fortune tellers who use this method of calculation use a special computerized program to ensure that no mistakes are made. This is because the combinations are said to be infinite.

My recommendation is to energize all the elements within the personal space. This means all the corners of the home so that you can ensure that the five elements of the home are in balance with no single element dominating. It is also an excellent idea to keep yin and yang nicely balanced for the same reason. All these tips are aimed at achieving these two fundamentals of feng shui practice.

Five Elements

The five elements are wood, fire, water, earth and metal. The elements interact according to their productive or their destructive cycles.

The productive cycle describes wood producing fire which produces earth which produces metal which produces water which produces wood in a never-ending cycle.

The destructive cycle describes wood as destroying earth which destroys water which destroys fire which destroys metal which destroys wood in a never-ending cycle.

Any element combination where one produces the other is harmonious. You can achieve this without having to resort to the Four Pillars calculation. Using the Compass formula methods to determine

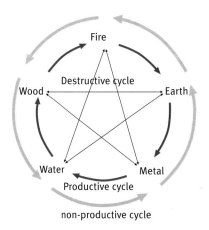

your auspicious directions is sufficient (see Tip 2). The directions and their elements are as follows: East and South-east are wood; South is fire; North is water; West and North-west are metal; and South-west and North-east are earth.

When you understand the basics of the five element cycle you can see how each one works together or can be destructive. In the productive cycle, metal produces water as shown here.

Memorizing Your Enhancing Elements

To personalize the feng shui of your interior décor, you can use the table on the right to identify the elements that are associated with different types of luck for you personally. This is based on your KUA number, which is calculated according to your date of birth and gender (see Tip 1). (For KUA number 5 the element above is for men, the one below for women.) Once you know which element is auspicious for different types of luck for you, memorize it, then incorporate it in soft furnishings, as patterns, colour, and shapes. Be creative using these guidelines:

- Metal element includes gold and silver. Circular designs reflect metal element. Colours are metallic and white.
- Water element is usually wavy and curved, suggesting waves, droplets and clouds. Colours are blue and black.
- Fire element is usually sharp, pointed and triangular. The sun motif is fire. Colours are red, orange and bright yellows.
- Wood element is usually rectangular and includes trees, plants and flowers – colours are brown and green.
- Earth element is square in shape, and the colours are beige and light yellow.

Auspicious Elements Based on Your KUA Number

Your KUA Number	1	2	3	4	5	6	7	8	9
Your success element	small wood	small earth	fire	water	small earth big earth	small metal	big metal	big earth	big wood
Your health element	big wood	small metal	water	fire	small metal big metal	small earth	big earth	big metal	small wood
Your romance element	fire	big metal	small wood	big wood	big metal small metal	big earth	small earth	small metal	water
Your education element	water	big earth	small wood	big wood	big earth small earth	big metal	small metal	small earth	fire

By looking at the chart above you can work out the best element colours and shapes for you to use. Here, wood is represented by the green cushion and rectangular rug and metal is the round plate.

12 Identify Your Destructive Elements

In the same way that you have auspicious elements that do 'special' things for your luck, every individual also has elements that are deemed to be 'destructive' to their good fortune. Each individual has four bad luck elements in ascending order of seriousness and gravity. These are presented in the table to the right. For KUA number 5, the element above is for men, the one below for women.

Inauspicious Elements Based on Your KUA Number

			Your KUA Number					
1	**2**	**3**	**4**	**5**	**6**	**7**	**8**	**9**
Your bad luck element								
small metal	big wood	big earth	big metal	big wood fire	small wood	water	fire	small earth
Your five ghosts element								
small earth	small wood	big metal	big earth	small wood water	big wood	fire	water	small metal
Your six killings element								
big metal	fire	small metal	small metal	fire big wood	water	small wood	small wood	big earth
Your total loss element								
big earth	water	small earth	small earth	water small wood	fire	big wood	small wood	big metal

Inauspicious Elements

The elements deemed 'destructive' under this KUA formula may well contradict what you discover to be elements you need, or are deemed lucky for you under another feng shui formula. When confronted with a situation where advice appears contradictory, it is important to understand that elements in and of themselves alone seldom do much harm. Simply refrain from energizing the destructive elements indicated. There is no need to use designs and colours that symbolize these elements for your own personal space. Thus if big wood is deemed inauspicious for you do not use green or wooden panelling in your part of the home or office.

Remember that the destructive elements indicated here refer only to your personal space, and not to your clothes.

A lush, green, healthy plant is a good representation of the wood element.

If wood is deemed inauspicious based on your KUA number and the table, and you were born in a wood year for instance, wearing green would still be regarded as auspicious for you although having wood symbols or green in your personal space would be bad. Such are the subtleties of the place of elements in feng shui practice.

Remember also that this table identifies your personal bad luck elements. Use them only for your own personal space – not for the whole house. Also, always factor in the destructive and productive cycles analysis (see Tip 10). Thus any element that produces an element that is deemed unlucky for you is also bad!

Keep Some Goldfish… or Some Carp

A truly great way of activating excellent feng shui luck inside the home is to keep some goldfish in an aquarium. Keep nine goldfish, of which eight should be red or golden and one should be black. If your goldfish die on you, do not fret. Simply get some more and replenish the aquarium. When one's fish die it is believed that they have absorbed some bad luck that was meant for a resident of the household.

However do not keep goldfish in the bedroom, in the toilets or in the kitchen. They are especially harmful in the bedroom as they can cause you to suffer some material losses. You could end up being burgled or robbed. Keep your aquarium either in the living room or position it outside the front of your house.

Goldfish bring a lot of luck in feng shui. Place an aquarium with odd numbers of them, including one that is black in the living room in a good location.

Your Best Aquarium Location

From now until the year 2003, the best location to keep a goldfish aquarium is in the East, South-east, North or South-west. To identify the absolute best location also depends on the direction your front door faces, and the formula is too complicated to present here. Just make sure you do not keep goldfish any where other than in those four locations. Water features are very tricky in feng shui. Get it right and it brings enormous luck. Get it wrong and it becomes very dangerous. A third rule is to never place your water feature, and especially a carp pond on the right-hand side of your main door (i.e. taking the direction from the inside facing outwards) since this causes the man of the house to have a roving eye!

14 Display Auspicious Calligraphy

The Chinese of olden days loved displaying auspicious calligraphy in their homes – and especially the character 'fook', shown below, which means luck. Almost all Chinese ancestral homes throughout Asia, especially those belonging to wealthy Chinese families, have their own versions of auspicious calligraphy. This symbolism of extreme good fortune is believed to be a very potent feng shui feature. There are those who even believe that the word 'fook' should also be displayed upside down to enhance the turnover of businesses.

Combining Symbols and Elements

Sometimes the auspicious calligraphy may be combined with other auspicious symbols like fish and water motifs. If water is an element that is auspicious for you, either because of your KUA number, or because you were born in a year when the heavenly stem was water or wood, then combining the word 'fook' with water and fish could bring you some good fortune.

Above Displaying some beneficial calligraphy on the walls has long been practised in China.

Left The 'fook' luck symbol is widely used as it is thought to bring good fortune to the people who use it.

Calligraphy and symbols can be hung as specially commissioned paintings, or carved on to wood blocks or furniture, inlaid with mother of pearl.

The carp is an especially auspicious symbol to display around the home. This is because the carp symbolizes ambition as well as the potential for attaining great heights in material success and power. The carp is also believed to have the ability to transform into the magnificent dragon.

Hang a Painting of Peonies For Love

The peony is regarded as the 'king of flowers' and symbolic of great good fortune associated with women. Legend has it that the famous Yang Kuei Fei, reputed to be the most beautiful woman in Chinese history and concubine to the Emperor, decorated her bedchamber with beautiful peony flowers all through the year. Because the Emperor could deny her nothing these flowers had to be specially brought to her from the South.

Activate Your Romance Luck

It is believed that if there is a family of girls and the mother wants them to marry well and find good husbands, then hanging a large picture of many peonies in the living room brings this kind of luck to the family. The living room is the best place for paintings of peonies, and the more luscious the blooms, the more magnificent will be the good fortune. Obviously if you can get hold of real peonies they would be just as auspicious, if not better. In my living room, I activate the South corner with huge pots of silk peonies, just as much for decoration as to create wonderful romantic luck for my daughter. If you are a single girl of marriageable age and you want to find a good husband then hang a peony just outside your bedroom door. You may also hang the painting inside your bedroom, but outside is better.

If you are already married, hanging a painting of peonies inside your bedroom will make your husband more amorous. The danger here is that he could well develop a roving eye and start to develop a love interest outside the marriage especially if the marriage is already getting boring. So be careful. I suggest if you have a peony painting, hang it in the living room – not in the bedroom. There are other less risky methods of bringing romance back into the marriage.

Images of peonies or the real flowers are believed to encourage romance for single women. They can be placed in the romance direction in the living room, or a picture can be hung just outside the bedroom door.

16

Create Good Luck With the Right Colours

Personalized interior decoration with feng shui is very much about the selection of colours, and the ways these colours are combined with each other. Different colours work best for different corners of the home or room.

Generally, the safest way to utilize colour in feng shui is to use the following table which gives you the dominant and secondary colours as well as those colours which should be strenuously avoided, in each of the corners of a home. Use the sketch below to help you identify the corners of your home.

Corners and Colours

CORNER	Dominant colours	Secondary colour	Taboo colour
SOUTH	red, orange	yellow, green	black, blue
NORTH	black, blue	white, metallic	yellow, beige
EAST	green, brown	black, blue	white, metallic
WEST	white, grey	metallic, yellow	red, orange
SOUTH-EAST	light green	light blue	grey, white
SOUTH-WEST	yellow, beige	red, orange	green, brown
NORTH-EAST	yellow, beige	red, orange	green, brown
NORTH-WEST	white, metallic	grey, yellow	red, orange

Interior Decor

This three-dimensional layout sketch of the different rooms in a two-storey house shows how you can work out the different corners of a home according the compass directions. Simply superimpose a nine-grid rectangle over the house (as shown by the black lines on the top of the house) to work out the different corners. Then use a compass to mark out the directions of each of the eight outer grids of the Lo Shu (ignore the middle one) which has been superimposed on the layout plan.The same directional sections will apply to each level of the house.

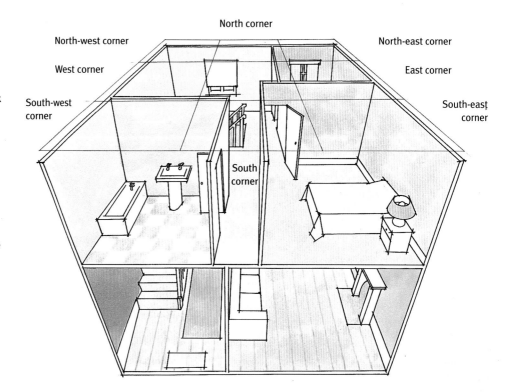

North-west corner
North corner
North-east corner
West corner
East corner
South-west corner
South-east corner
South corner

Grow an Orange or Lime Plant

An orange or lime tree weighed down heavily with ripening fruits symbolizes rising good fortune and prosperity. Such plants are usually displayed at the entrances to doors of Chinese homes and office buildings during the fifteen days of the lunar new year to signify a prosperous start to the year.

The connotation of bright red oranges also signifies gold because the sound of the word for oranges 'kum' also means gold. It is thus considered extreme good fortune to have plenty of oranges around during the new year. Having a fruiting orange plant is even more auspicious.

If you grow an orange plant in your garden, plant it in the South-east because this is the corner of your home that symbolizes wealth. Having a healthy fruiting orange plant there is extremely auspicious.

Solving Direction Problems

Please do not worry if the South-east happens to be your 'total loss' direction and location. When you energize or activate a corner to create the luck which that direction symbolizes, it brings that particular good fortune to all residents. As long as you personally do not have your room in the South-east, or sit facing the South-east, you will also benefit. Remember that all the different methods of feng shui must complement each other. When the recommendations seem to be contradicting each other, think through the problem. The solution is usually not difficult.

If you are a keen gardener you might wish to know that almost all plants bring good fortune to the home when they bloom and are robust. However, chrysanthemums, bamboo, orchids, and plum blossoms are specifically mentioned in feng shui textbooks as being especially auspicious.

A laden orange tree symbolizes the arrival of good fortune and prosperity. Placing one in the South-east corner of your garden is auspicious as this is your wealth area.

18 The Feng Shui of Plants in the Home

Cactus Plants

Do avoid placing cactus plants inside the office or the home. No matter how tempting the beautiful cactus blooms are, they do not compensate for the bad energy created by the deadly thorns of the plants. When placed in the home or office (on windowsills and ledges) prickly cactus plants always create tiny slivers of poisonous energy that, over time, cause illness, misfortunes and losses.

Cactus plants are best placed outside the home or office where they take on the symbolic role of sentinel protectors. The thorns serve as an effective countering force against shar chi or 'killing breath' entering the home or office.

Try not to place bonsai plants in the home as they represent stunted growth.

When cactus plants are put in the garden they give protection to your home. But do not keep them inside as bad energy is thought to be created by the sharp thorns.

Bonsai Plants

These plants represent stunted growth and, for this reason, are not good feng shui. I do not mean artistically pruned shrubs and plants as these actually bring great good energy to the home and office. What I mean are varieties of large trees that have been cleverly and artificially stunted over many years, and are usually worth a great deal of money. These genuine bonsai plants are extremely valuable.However, they are not good feng shui as they signify blocks to one's growth and to one's business. If you must have them, place them in the North where they cause least harm.

If you have a passion for bonsai and absolutely must have them in your home or garden, I suggest you avoid placing them in the wood corners of the home or garden. This means the East or the South-east. Placed in the North, they cause the least harm.

Create Curtains That Bring Good Luck

19

Curtains and all the soft furnishings of the home or office can be designed to enhance the feng shui of your personal space. One of the easiest ways of doing this is to be sensitive to the elements that should be energized in the different corners of any room (see p.16). The first thing to do is determine what sort of room you are dealing with. Then, look at the table below to check on the most auspicious curtain colours.

In a West room, white curtains are excellent. White, which is suggestive of the metal element, is superb for the West. Curtains that are dominantly circular and round in shape also reflect the element of metal. This means the curtains are most auspicious because they have been correctly blended in with the element of the corner the room occupies. Two layers of curtains are ideal for 'deflecting' excessive yang energy of the afternoon sun, which shines into the West corner of any home.

In a bedroom that is located in the North corner of the home, the auspicious element will be water. Thus, blue curtains are very suitable. Circular curtain pelmets suggest metal and this is excellent because metal produces water. Tiny wavy pleats in the curtain also suggests water, which complements the theme of the element of the North. Please note that energizing elements in this way is different from placing physical water or hanging paintings of water in the bedroom.

Using Element Analysis

You can use element analysis to help you create balance throughout your home. But

Guide to Curtains Depending on Corner

These curtains with a triangular pelmet design can be hung in a room in the South (fire).

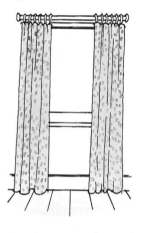

These long rectangular curtains are suitable for a room in the East (wood).

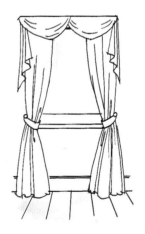

These curtains with their rolled design are for a room in the West (metal).

These curtains with their scalloped pelmet and wavy fabric combine the metal and water element and can be hung in the North.

you should also note the various taboos along the way. For example, do not ever place aquariums or plants in the bedroom as they are not auspicious.

Sleep on an Authentic Feng Shui Bed

An auspicious feng shui bed is decorated in colours that harmonize with the sleeper's year element or the element of the corner in which it is placed. Thus, if you were born in a fire year, then shades of red would suit you, but not too red. Or, if your bed were placed in the East corner of the bedroom, then shades of green would be very suitable. When in doubt on which system to use, I follow the element of the corner. This makes the bed generally auspicious for both my husband and I since we have different year elements. If your bed is in the fire corner be careful that you do not make the fire element too strong. Too much yang energy in the bedroom is bad for sleep.

Bedspreads

Bedspreads that are dark in colour are to be preferred over lighter ones. Plain, coloured bedspreads are also better than patterned designs if you are unsure of what could be harmful. Generally, however, I warn against selecting bedspread designs that have abstract prints or patterns with triangular or pointed symbols. Such fire-related symbolism is usually discouraged for the bedroom, which is supposed to be a place of rest. Fire transmits yang energy, which is not so suitable for sleep. In the bedroom it would be preferable to allow yin energies to dominate, although not to an extent that can be harmful.

This bed has been placed in the West of the bedroom so the wall has been painted white to complement the element. The bedspread is also white (metal) with black (water) trimming which is perfectly acceptable as metal produces water. However, the mirror in the picture should be moved as it reflects the bed which is bad feng shui.

Let Your Carpets Create Solid Foundations

The feng shui of your floor relates to the foundation of your life. This principle has important feng shui connotations when it comes to personalized interior decoration.

The Ground Rules

Firstly, let all your carpets blend with the elements of the room in which they are placed. This depends on the compass direction corner of the room. The ruling element then helps you choose the colour and pattern of your carpet (see Tip 10).

Secondly, except with wall-to-wall carpeting, let carpets reflect the general shape of the room. This creates balance and harmony. In the picture is a carpet that mirrors the energy and shape of most rooms thereby allowing the room's foundations to be firmly in line with the rest of the room. This suggests that rectangular carpets are always to be preferred to round or oval carpets.

Thirdly, do not have carpets with busy patterns and designs. These cause confused energies. Carpets that have exquisite and elaborate detailing (e.g. the stunning Persians) are not to be included in this category. It is the abstract designs that can create masses of uncertainty, which in turn can cause problems.

It is best to avoid buying carpets or rugs that have very exaggerated, abstract designs but Persian carpets with their intricate detailing are fine to use.

Finally, do not place carpets on the wall. An object that is generally associated with the ground is best left on ground. This guideline becomes especially important to observe if many different people have stepped upon the exquisite carpet you have just bought while it was still in the shop. If it is an antique masterpiece, the provenance and history of which you know nothing about, you need to be even more careful. To hang such a carpet on your wall could well bring accumulated negative vibrations into your home. So be careful.

22 | Feng Shui Tips on Flowers in the Home

In the living room fresh flowers create refreshing yang energy which brings good vibes into the home. Flowers are very useful in creating good feng shui, but there are some basic guidelines you should observe.

Fresh flowers should be thrown out as soon as they start to fade as anything dead or decaying creates an excess of negative yin energy. For this reason I always advise against displaying or using dried flowers in flower arrangements. I would rather have fake flowers than dried flowers since the fake flowers symbolize yang and life energy while the dried flowers represent yin and dead energy.

Yang Energy

Flowers can be used to enhance or reduce the yang energies of a room. Generally speaking, flowers do not bring suitable feng shui for bedrooms. They are better suited to living rooms and dining rooms.

Just as I do not recommend the use of flowers for enhancing the feng shui of any bedroom, in the same way I would not suggest the placing of live plants in the bedroom. This is because flowers and plants bring yang energies into the bedroom, and this often makes the room excessively yang and so not conducive to peaceful sleep. However, because fresh flowers are so yang, they are extremely suitable for the bedroom of sick or convalescing people. In such a situation flowers are excellent for the bedroom and the giving of such flowers is also considered auspicious, bringing as it does some precious yang energy to the recipient.

Flowers, whether displayed singly (above) or in bunches (left), give out good yang energy in living areas. But always throw out the flowers as soon as they start to wilt as dead flowers are very negative.

Hang Feng Shui Coins or Bells on Door Handles

This is one of my personal favourite things to do in order to attract auspicious money luck into my home. As a result everyone living in my home benefits, including the maid and gardener. I hang three Chinese coins on the door handles of my main doors – the kind that have the square holes in the centre – tied together with red string which activates the essence of good fortune symbolized by the coins. The coins hang on the inside of my doors and are thus deemed to be already inside my home!

Another good tip is also to hang a small bell on the door handle. But the bell should be hung outside the door. The bell is different from the coins. Its sound is believed to entice good fortune luck to come to the home whereas the coins represent wealth that has already come into the home.

In following this tip there is no need to go overboard and hang these coins on every single door in your home. Indeed, whenever you overdo any feng shui recommendation, the results can often turn from positive to negative. Never forget that feng shui is about balance. So limit the application of this tip to your main front door.

Focus on the Main Door

You should never hang any coins or the feng shui-energizing symbol on the back door. In feng shui, the back door represents the way out for you. To create good fortune feng shui it is sufficient to focus on the main front door.

This tip is particularly potent when your main front door happens to be located in the West or North-west of your home. This is because both the coins and the bell symbolize the metal, which is the element of these two directions.

Hanging three Chinese coins threaded with red ribbon or cotton on the door handles of your main doors can bring good fortune into your home.

Watch Where You Position Your Cooker

In the kitchen layout, the hob or oven should never be placed next to the sink. In the picture above the sink is on the opposite side of the island unit so does not face the oven. In the picture on the left the hob and oven are not situated directly next to the sink.

Many Compass School methods of feng shui strongly warn against the family's stove (or cooker) being placed in the North-west of the kitchen or the home. To be on the safe side, I advise against having the kitchen in the North-west, but if your kitchen is placed there, then you must at least make certain your stove or cooker is not in the North-west corner of your kitchen.

The North-west is the corner that is said to represent the father of the family or bread-winner. If you place the cooker there you are burning their luck and there can be nothing worse than destroying the breadwinner's luck.

'Fire at Heaven's Gate'

The North-west also represents 'heaven' so having the cooker here suggests 'fire at heaven's gate' and there is nothing more inauspicious than this. It is said that, at worst, having the stove in this part of the kitchen causes the family's wealth to be wasted. At best, it causes the house to be completely razed. This is a serious feng shui defect which should be corrected. Remember that the stove represents fire, which is the only element capable of destroying the metal element of the North-west (see Tip 10).

The second major point about kitchen arrangements is to watch out for the clash between fire (stove/oven/cooker) and water (refrigerator, dishwasher and sink). These two elements should neither be placed next to each other, nor should they confront each other. This latter arrangement has water opposite fire! The direct confrontation orientation is more harmful than having the two elements side by side.

Place Hi-fi Equipment Along the West Wall

25

All stereo and hi-fi equipment brings extra good luck to the house when placed against the West wall of the living room. Equipment placed in the West creates the potential for huge good fortune that will ripen starting from the year 2003. The good fortune will last for 20 years.

Hi-fi equipment signifies the metal element, which is excellent for the West sector of the living room.

Keep your television sets in the living room or family room. If you have a TV in your bedroom, cover it with a cloth before you go to sleep. A television set directly facing the bed creates extremely bad chi (or energy) for the couple and causes husband and wife, or lovers, to be separated for long periods of time. Television sets facing the bed are similar in effect to mirrors. Misfortune that creates severe unhappiness can result.

Keep Brooms and Mops Out of Sight

26

You will never see brooms, mops and other cleaning paraphernalia in a traditional Chinese home, especially those homes where the mother of the family is very strong. Those of the older generation who grew up on a diet of cultural superstition consider it extremely inauspicious to see brooms around the home instead of being kept hidden away. Exposed brooms are especially forbidden in dining rooms. The presence of exposed brooms here will 'sweep away the family's rice bowl and livelihood', and is thus considered bad feng shui.

Keep Intruders at Bay

Here is an unusual tip passed on to me years ago by someone in Hong Kong. In the early years of my nine-year stay in Hong Kong I was neurotic about security, and went to elaborate pains to install burglar alarm systems. These super-sensitive installations often led to

false alarms and embarrassing moments with the local police in the middle of the night.

I was then advised by a feng shui consultant, who happened to be the father of one of my own bank employees that the best way to keep intruders away was to lean a broom upside down against the wall and facing the front door. This would keep out unwanted visitors. If you want to use this tip, place the broom outside the home, not on the inside. Keep the broom there during the nocturnal hours. In the daytime keep the broom out of sight.

Mops and brooms are associated with the 'sweeping' out of the negative and stale energy of the home, but should always be kept out of sight.

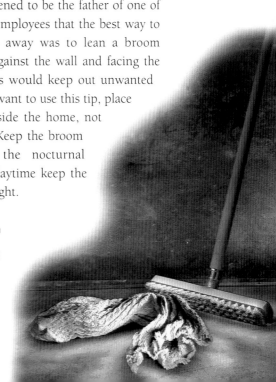

27

Do Not Over-decorate Your Toilets

Ever since I became an avid fan of feng shui, I have strenuously warned my wealthy friends against spending too much money making the toilets and bathrooms of their house their pride and joy. These rooms are a part of the home that have the greatest potential to create havoc with your feng shui.

Toilets Create Bad Feng Shui

Toilet and bathroom fittings are horrendously expensive, yet many people like their toilets and bathroom very large and well-equipped. This is a big mistake, because toilets create bad feng shui in whatever corner they are located. The actual type of bad luck depends on which corner is 'afflicted'. Chinese homes

Be careful not to over-decorate your toilet as this area always drains away energy from your home.

long ago rarely had toilets. Night soil carriers took away the family's waste material. The rich had their baths brought in by servants. And even poor peasants had their toilets built some way away from the home.

For modern living I advise toilets to be made small, hidden away, and always kept closed. It is also not necessary to decorate the toilet with paintings, flowers, antiques and other toilet paraphernalia. Do not place auspicious flowers and symbols in the toilet as this can sometimes cause severe problems in the area of life which you are desperately trying to correct.

Let me tell you a story. I had a friend whose toilet was located in the children's corner (in the West). Her children's grades suffered and they endured one disappointment after another. Nothing they did could succeed. I told her to place a mirror on the toilet door to make the toilet symbolically disappear. This worked. Both the children graduated with excellent grades. Both found good jobs. And then my friend started to place flowers in her toilet – fake peonies and plum blossoms – to energize her children's corner. She forgot she was energizing her toilet. The peonies were supposed to bring romance luck to her daughter.

Her daughter did find romance and love but with a good-for-nothing boy who brought nothing but heartache to the family. It was only after the toilet was completely cleared of the flowers that her daughter came to her senses and discarded the objectionable young man. So be careful!

Dissolve the Shar Chi of Open Shelves

Open bookshelves resemble knives that send out the shar chi or 'killing breath' into the room. Whether these shelves are in your home or your office, my advice is to dissolve the shar chi created by putting doors on to them. The effect of open shelves may not be felt immediately but residents of rooms with open shelves almost always succumb eventually – usually to illnesses that can prove fatal.

I have seen many large offices of corporate bosses where the shelves have been placed on three walls to make the room fit the interior decorator's idea of an important corporate office. I can only say that such shelves can cause the occupant of the room to succumb to a heart attack. Sadly, I have seen this happen in several instances.

In circumstances where you really cannot do anything about the exposed shelves in your office or room, the next best thing is to arrange your books to sit 'flush' with the blades of the shelves. This symbolically makes the shelves disappear, and can be done with books and with large files.

It is not possible to use this method for shelves displaying decorative items. In this situation you might want to sandpaper the edges of the shelves. This in effect 'blunts' the cutting sharpness of the shelves and does alleviate the situation somewhat.

Finally it might be useful to note that glass shelves are particularly harmful in the North corners while wooden shelves are harmful in the South-west, the North-east as well as the centre of any room. Plastic shelves are the least harmful of all.

Open shelf units take on the appearance of knives. But by standing books flush to the edges you can help to reduce the bad effects.

A Family Room to Create Harmony

This tip looks at the placement of rooms in the overall layout of your home. If you examine the layout plans of the two houses below you will note that the family rooms of each are in different locations. The family room in the first house is in the centre and is thus more conducive to family harmony than the location of the family room in the second plan. The dotted lines are the imaginary lines of a Lo Shu square superimposed on the layout plan. A Lo Shu square is a nine-sector grid, which is used as a feng shui tool, (see Tip 16).

In this case we are using the square to help in determining the centre of the home. It is very easy to see if the family room is in the centre grid of the Lo Shu. If so, the room is auspicious for the family. There will be goodwill amongst family members and husband and wife will stay on good terms. Children will tend to be more obedient and siblings will stay close to each other.

A staircase in the centre is bad! If the staircase is spiral this 'bores' into the heart of the home. If placed in the centre, curved or straight staircases are not as damaging as spiral staircases. If you have a centre staircase do not carpet it in red or green.

Kitchens and bedrooms should not be in the centre of the home since this lays undue importance on eating and sleeping. A kitchen in the centre presses down on the entire family's good fortune. You should relocate the kitchen if you have this kind of layout.

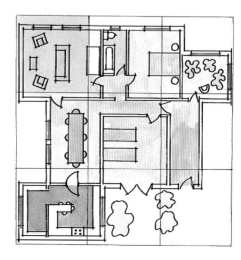

Good Room Placement

The Lo Shu square has been placed on these two diagrams to show the centre of the home. In the diagram above, the family room is situated in the centre which is good for harmonious living but, in the one on the right, it is in the top-left corner and is not as auspicious.

Happy Family Portraits Bring Togetherness

One of the best and most effective methods of creating a sense of family togetherness is to hang a large family portrait in a place of honour in the living room or family room. Every member of the family should be included in the portrait and, to symbolize happiness, every member should be smiling. Arrange the members of the family in a way that creates a shape most suitable to the element of the father of the family.

Good Family Pictures

For a family of five people the triangular shape is just as auspicious to use as it indicates the the element of fire and the presence of good yang energy.

Four people in a picture suggests the shape of a square, which is the earth element. This also relates to family so is a suitable shape for everyone.

Triangular Arrangement

If you choose this arrangement, make sure the breadwinner or father of the family is placed at the apex of the triangle. This particular arrangement creates the element of fire, and it also signifies the precious yang energy. It is particularly appropriate when the father of the family was born in a fire or earth year. I have used this arrangement for my own family portrait.

Wavy Arrangement

This arrangement creates the water element. It is a yin shape and is great if there is excessive yang energy in the home in the form of many male relatives. The father or breadwinner should be in the centre, and the heads of the people in the picture not level, creating a wavy shape. This is excellent when the father was born in a water or wood year.

Rectangular Arrangement

This arrangement suggests the wood element, and is probably the most common. Here, all members pose in a way that has everyone's head level. The arrangement also suggests a regular, balanced shape. It is suitable when the father was born in a wood or fire year.

Square Arrangement

This is similar to the rectangle and is especially suited for small families. For instance, four in a picture makes a perfect square, a shape that suggests the earth element. This arrangement is suitable for everyone since the earth element also signifies the family. It is also good if the father was born in a metal year since earth produces metal in the cycle of the elements (see Tip 10).

31 Mandarin Ducks to Enhance Your Love Life

Mandarin ducks are to feng shui what lovebirds are to Western cultures. You will find these ducks are depicted in many items of Chinese arts and crafts. This is because a pair of mandarin ducks is regarded as a symbol of romance, love and fidelity for young couples.

Placed in the South-west corners of bedrooms or of the home these ducks create energies that greatly enhance your love life. If you're single, hang a painting of these ducks, or get a pair of carved wooden ducks from the Chinese emporium and place them in your bedroom. Make sure you put a pair, not one or three, since the connotation of one is that you will stay stubbornly single, and that of three implies a marriage or love relationship that could well get crowded! Also, if you want to attract the opposite sex, then do make certain that you place a male and female in a pair – not two males or two females together. Please ask the shop assistant to tell you the difference between the male duck and the female duck.

Lovebirds

If you are not able to find any mandarin ducks, please use the modern equivalent of the lovebird, but again make sure you display a pair of birds. The birds can also be included in the form of a painting or picture. Do not attempt to keep the real thing. I must hasten to say that, as a general rule, I discourage keeping any birds in cages as I regard this as bad feng shui. This is because caged birds symbolize an inability to 'fly' – or to grow one's ambitions.

Mandarin ducks represent love and romance, so a wallhanging like the one illustrated can be placed in the South-west corner of your bedroom or your home.

Mirrors in the Bedroom Cause Problems

irrors possess a special form of energy which can either be very good or very bad. The one place where mirrors can do a great deal of harm is in the bedroom. Mirrors are a major taboo in the bedroom. Here, mirrors cause havoc in a couple's marriage and love life. Mirrors are often responsible for the entrance of third parties into an otherwise good relationship. If you must have a mirror in your bedroom, keep it closed, or covered during sleep. No mirrors on the ceiling please!

One should be very careful about mirrors that directly face the bed. This can happen when built-in cupboards have mirror doors that directly reflect the bed. Feng shui masters attribute the breakdown of marriages, and especially infidelity, to the negative effect of mirrors reflecting the bed. In feng shui lore the reason given is that the mirror creates energies which then disturb the relationship of the sleeping couple.

The bedroom is the room we occupy during the long nocturnal hours and I prefer not to have mirrors anywhere near or reflecting me – far better to keep the mirrors out of sight when I sleep and am vulnerable.

This bedroom has bad feng shui for the couple as the mirror doors are at the side of the bed and these can cause problems in a relationship. However, there are curtains to the bed so the mirrors can be obscured from sight at night.

'Spirituality Cleansing'

Feng shui master, Mr Yap, also warns against mirrors. He maintains that the shock of suddenly seeing oneself reflected in the mirror upon waking up, can be so disturbing that negative energies are created for that person.

Mr Yap once described the ritual of 'spirituality cleansing' a place believed to be haunted or disturbed by wandering spirits. The ritual involved the use of a mirror to 'reflect' the spirit(s) into the mirror, after which the mirror itself was blessed in order to control the bad spirits. If this part of the ritual is not done properly, Mr Yap told me, the spirits stay trapped inside the mirror. Since hearing that sinister tale, I have been extra careful with mirrors.

33 Separate Mattresses Lead to Separation

If you want to take feng shui into consideration when planning your master bedroom, then you should make certain your double bed is really a double bed and that you have a single piece of mattress. You should never have two mattresses since this symbolically creates a schism between the sleeping couple. It is far better to have two separate beds, or even have separate bedrooms to take account of two people having different auspicious directions than to sleep on a bed which has two mattresses.

A double bed that has two mattresses is considered very bad for the future of a marriage as it will cause the couple eventually to separate.

Avoiding Conflict in the Bedroom

Two other bedroom features can cause a couple to split or have severe misunderstandings that lead to separation:

● A beam that is directly above the bed that symbolically splits the bed into two. If your bed is situated directly below such a beam (which is a bad configuration anyway) do try to move the bed out from under it. If you cannot do this then create a false ceiling that makes the beam symbolically disappear.

● If the bed's position lies between two doors that create an imaginary line cutting the bed into two, (and this is a very inauspicious arrangement anyway), you should either move the bed, or place a screen to obscure one door.

Left Sleeping under beams is not good feng shui, especially for a couple, as they can figuratively be cut in two. If the bed has to go under beams, you can use material to tent the area and solve the problem.

Don't Sleep Facing the Door

Left The best place to position your bed is diagonally opposite the door. Do not ever place your bed so that your feet face the door as this is considered to be a bad sleeping position.

According to Chinese custom the death position is when one has one's feet directly facing the door. The corpses of dead relatives are placed in this way prior to the funeral. This arrangement is deemed to be a very excellent yin position for the dead, but it is deadly for the living!

Positioning Your Bed

Actually, feng shui advises that neither the head nor the feet should be pointed directly at the door of the room. Thus, when positioning a bed, it always advisable to have it placed either to the left or right of the door.

If there is an attached or ensuite bathroom or toilet, it is important to make certain that the two doors, i.e. the entrance door and the toilet door, are not aligned in a straight line. It is even worse if the bed itself is sandwiched in-between them. In this case you

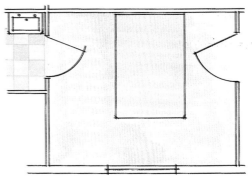

Right If the only way you can place your bed is between two doors as shown here, block out one of the doors with a screen.

need to place a screen or cabinet to block off one of the doors.

You also need to move the bed but do not end up having the bed pointed to either the toilet door or the entrance door. If your bedroom is very small and you have no choice then I advise that you place your bed with the headboard situated in one of the corners. This sort of irregular arrangement is perfectly acceptable.

35

A Few Tips for Childless Couples

One reason I am so enamoured of feng shui is that it really can bring enormous happiness to one's life. It is especially effective in helping couples who want children but seem to be having a hard time conceiving. I am not referring to those with medical problems. I am saying that if you have tried and checked everything and find there is nothing wrong with you, or your partner, and still you cannot conceive, then feng shui might be able to help. This was what happened to me.

My inability to conceive had been due to a huge poison arrow which took the form of a large casuarina tree not ten feet from my main door. This created bad shar chi (or 'killing breath') that hit my front door. We were childless for nine years! If you are having a hard time conceiving, it is a good idea to check whether anything sharp, pointed or threatening is hurting your main door or your bed! The chances are that you will find some-

If you really want children and are having problems conceiving, check that there are no poison arrows hitting your front door. Also move your bed into the auspicious nien yen corner of your bedroom.

thing. When you do, try to shield it or block it off from view, or you might consider moving out like we did. We moved to another house and designed our new home according to feng shui principles, concentrating on activating our descendants' luck.

● Please check the husband's nien yen direction based on the table given in Tip 2. Then try to occupy the bedroom that is located in his nien yen location. Next, position the bed so you both sleep in his nien yen direction. This activates his descendants' luck. In feng shui the effect of the women's descendants' luck is not counted.

● Look for a painting or picture of children and hang it in the vicinity of the bed. In the imperial palaces of the Forbidden City, the Emperor's conjugal bed is decorated with screens and embroidery of the famous '100 children' to symbolize great fertility in his encounters with his many wives.

● Find a young male virgin born in the year of the dragon and ask him to symbolically 'roll' across your bed. Ideally this should have been done on the wedding night, but better late than never. Or place a small representation of the dragon next to the bed to simulate precious yang energy.

Coping With Difficult Children

If you are having problems with your children, you must check the feng shui of your home. First you should walk through your house and investigate whether anything, any structure or object may be harming your front door or the beds and desks of your children. See if the door into the children's room is directly facing a toilet or a staircase. The negative energy created can cause the resident to feel listless, rebellious and completely lacking in motivation. Good yang energy is depleted. Try to change rooms for your child or hang a small windchime above the door between the door and the staircase or toilet.

Find Your Family-orientated Direction

If your problem is a teenager who is disobedient, who does not like coming home and who seems to have no sensitivity to the family then you must investigate his or her sleeping

If your teenage daughter insists on sleeping on the floor you will need to dissuade her.

direction. Check the KUA (see Tip 1) number and try to make him/her sleep with the head pointed to the nien yen direction (see the table in Tip 2). This is a family-oriented direction and will make a great deal of difference. We have helped a great many of our friends with their rebellious teenagers, just by using this one tip.

Try also to dissuade your son or daughter from sleeping on the floor, or on a bed so low as to be level with the floor. This is thought to be neither auspicious nor conducive to his/her personal happiness, instead they could become unsettled and there could also be a possibility of problems with health.

When the problem with your children has to do with study grades, their work could be suffering because of wrong sitting directions. For children, the direction to tap is their fu wei direction. Check what these directions are based on their date of birth and the table. Then let your child sleep with his/her head pointed in the fu wei direction and to work at a desk facing this direction too.

You should also hang or place a small crystal in the North-east corner of the bedroom. The crystal is an excellent education energizer that harmonizes very well with the North-east, which is also the education corner.

37

Attract Romance and Love With Crystals

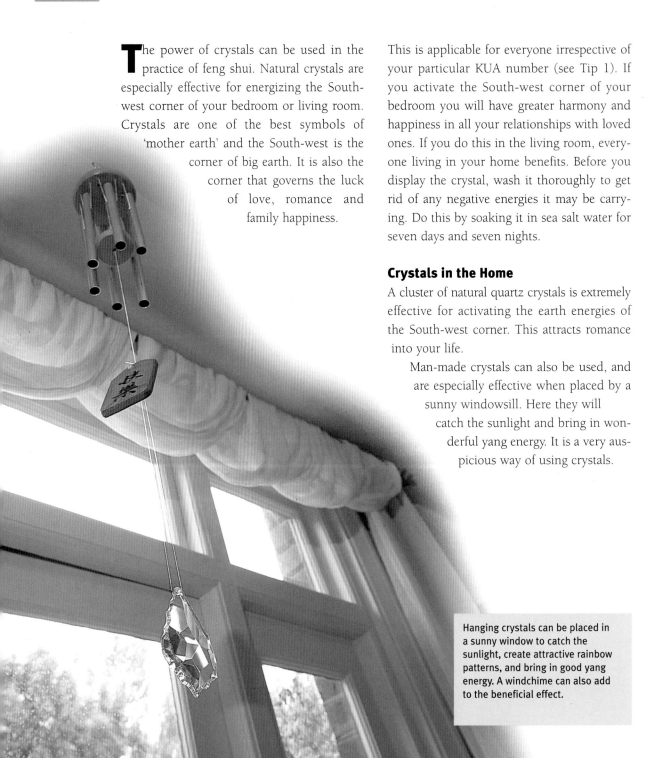

The power of crystals can be used in the practice of feng shui. Natural crystals are especially effective for energizing the South-west corner of your bedroom or living room. Crystals are one of the best symbols of 'mother earth' and the South-west is the corner of big earth. It is also the corner that governs the luck of love, romance and family happiness.

This is applicable for everyone irrespective of your particular KUA number (see Tip 1). If you activate the South-west corner of your bedroom you will have greater harmony and happiness in all your relationships with loved ones. If you do this in the living room, everyone living in your home benefits. Before you display the crystal, wash it thoroughly to get rid of any negative energies it may be carrying. Do this by soaking it in sea salt water for seven days and seven nights.

Crystals in the Home

A cluster of natural quartz crystals is extremely effective for activating the earth energies of the South-west corner. This attracts romance into your life.

Man-made crystals can also be used, and are especially effective when placed by a sunny windowsill. Here they will catch the sunlight and bring in wonderful yang energy. It is a very auspicious way of using crystals.

Hanging crystals can be placed in a sunny window to catch the sunlight, create attractive rainbow patterns, and bring in good yang energy. A windchime can also add to the beneficial effect.

Get Him/Her to Commit With Feng Shui

If your problem is getting your partner to make a commitment, to propose marriage, or simply to acknowledge you are an 'item' then, in addition to displaying a crystal in the South-west corner of love, you should give strength to the crystal by installing a very bright light there. The best feng shui energizer for this purpose is to hang a crystal chandelier in the South-west corner of the bedroom of the house, but any bright light, kept turned on for at least three hours every night would be helpful. It is unnecessary to overdo things by making the light too bright. Halogens and spotlights are much too harsh, and are not good feng shui.

Guard Your South-west

Sometimes the problem is created by the presence of a toilet in the South-west corner of the home. I have seen so many examples of this being the cause of my friends' children having a hard time getting married even though they were not lacking in suitors. If you have a toilet in the South-west that is spoiling your chances of getting married, my suggestion is for you to keep the toilet permanently locked. Stop using the toilet altogether and turn it into a store-room. If you cannot do this, the next best thing is to hang a five rod wind-chime that is made of wood and painted black or brown to 'press down' on the bad energy being created by the toilet. A way of making the toilet 'disappear' is to hang a full-length mirror on the door of the toilet.

Enhance Marriage Luck

Another good way to activate the wedding luck of people of marriageable age is to place a few large boulders in the South-west corner of the garden. Paint the double happiness symbol in red on the rock, or tie a piece of red string around the rock so that you activate its inherent energies.

Above For commitment in your relationship, try energizing your South-west bedroom corner with a crystal and a bright light.

Left You can also activate your wedding luck by painting the double happiness symbol on boulders in the South-west area of your garden.

Energizing Your Love Corners

In addition to the following general feng shui tips on love and romance, you can also energize and protect your personalized nien yen direction and location. Check your personal nien yen direction by referring to the table in Tip 2; then try to achieve at least three of the following to describe your personal space. It is never possible to get everything correctly aligned to suit your personalized direction but as long as you get about 60 to 70 per cent right, your feng shui will work in your favour.

To improve your love life you can energize your own nien yen corner in your bedroom by following the tips on the chart on the right.

- Sleep with your head pointed to your nien yen direction.
- Choose a bedroom which is in your nien yen corner.
- Make sure your toilet is not in your nien yen corner.
- Let your bedroom door face your nien yen direction.
- Make sure your nien yen corner is not missing.

If your nien yen is South
Hang a bright light in the South corner of your bedroom. Then place a small red light in the North-west corner, and hang a windchime in the North-east.

If your nien yen is South-east
Place a small red light in the South-east of your bedroom. Then hang a windchime in the North-east and place another red light in the North-west.

If your nien yen is East
Place a small red light in the East. Then decorate the West of your bedroom with something red, and the South-west with something black.

If your nien yen is North-west
Place a silver picture frame in the North-west. Then decorate the east and South-east in metallic or grey.

If your nien yen is South-west
Place a red light or crystals in the South-west of your bedroom. Place crystals in the North corner and decorate the East in metallic colours.

If your nien yen is North-east
Place a red light or crystals in the North-east and decorate the East and South-east of your bedroom in metallic or grey colours.

If your nien yen is West
Have a golden or silver coloured bedspread and hang a silver-framed photo on the West wall of the bedroom. Then place crystals in the North corner.

If your nien yen is North
Display something small that is painted black in the North part of your bedroom. Then decorate the West and South-west in metallic or grey colours.

Beware Exclusively Male/Female Energies

If you want to find a partner, if you wish to get married, if you want the happiness of romance and family life, if you really do not want to be alone, then the first thing to do is go around your home and see if you are displaying anything that symbolizes a single gender. If you are a woman, check to see if your paintings are all of women. If you hang nothing but females on the walls of your home, it is unlikely that your home can attract 'male' energy. This situation is not as unlikely as it seems. I have visited enough single girlfriends to find nothing but beautiful paintings of women on their walls. My girlfriends were not gay, but just art lovers who appreciated the female form and completely forgot to create balance in the display of their artwork.

I had another friend who had the same problem. Robert was a very nice iconoclastic English male bachelor who lived alone in a stunning apartment on the Peak in Hong Kong. At one of his dinner parties I noticed that his home had nothing but stereotypical 'male decorations'. There were pictures of cricket stars and paintings of naval heroes. There were Sotheby's type sculptures of men and busts of dead poets. There was nothing that suggested anything feminine. His home was completely too 'yang' by far. When he confided he was having no luck with women, I told him about the lack of female energy in his home. Robert changed this by adding two marvellous paintings of the female form. The resulting balance of energies has long since created a happy ending for Robert and his wife Natalie.

One Hundred Beauties of Suchou

A passionately professional girlfriend of mine had a huge reproduction of the famous Chinese painting entitled *One Hundred Beauties of Suchou*, a classic painting commissioned by the Ching Emperor Chien Lung, centuries ago, in celebration of the beautiful women of Suchou. This beautiful painting, rendered in silk, hung in her living room. She confided to me one day that nothing would make her happier than to get married and raise a family. 'But I don't seem to be able to keep any relationship going for longer than two months,' she laughed. Then going on 38 years old, she admitted she was getting desperate. I checked her nien yen and told her about feng shui.

I persuaded her to give away her *One Hundred Beauties* painting explaining that the female yin energies created by all those women in that painting was much too powerful. She balked at first but later presented it to her brother as a birthday gift. Shortly afterwards, she met Brian who proposed after a three-month courtship. Today, eleven years later, they are still happily married.

Unlucky in love ?
By having a good balance of male and female art in your living areas, you are more likely to encourage a relationship if you are single.

41 Keep Things in Pairs

If you don't like being alone and want someone to share your life, you would be well advised to surround your personal space with things that symbolize Nature's uncontrived pairing of the male with the female. The ultimate symbol of Chinese feng shui is the yin/yang symbol which encapsulates the complementary nature of the male/female union. This represents the balance that is so vital in feng shui symbolism.

Two For Luck

The Chinese are extremely conscious of the auspiciousness of giving, taking or displaying things in pairs. Many of the prosperity and good luck symbols of the Chinese come in pairs – the ultimate of which is, of course, the dragon. Dragons are either shown in pairs – two dragons frolicking with the eternal pearl, or a dragon and a phoenix to symbolize conjugal happiness.

Paired objects can also bring you romance. The mandarin ducks above can help encourage young love, while the yin and yang balls below symbolize the ultimate union between man and woman.

Mandarin ducks, which symbolize the happiness of young love, are also always shown in pairs. Whether drawn on to ceramics or depicted as brush paintings, they are never featured alone. Neither will you ever see three in a painting. Another symbol of love is a pair of butterflies, although this is seldom used in feng shui since this is a symbol of a love that ends in tragedy. The Chinese folk tale of the star-crossed lovers who die in each other's arms and are reunited as butterflies is a well-known one. However, even this symbol of tragic love is still shown as a pair.

Two other extremely meaningful and auspicious symbols are the double fish, which is a very lucky symbol and the pair of footsteps which signify Buddha's footsteps. This is also a religious symbol for Buddhists of all traditions, and it expresses the karmic happiness of prosperous rebirths that occur after death.

Happiness Décor For the Bedroom

The conventional feng shui advice for bedrooms is that, since it is a place of rest, colours should be more suggestive of yin, rather than yang energies, although never to such an extent that there is imbalance.

For happiness luck in one's love relationship, however, feng shui does prescribe the use of warmer, yang colours. In the old days this was usually related to fertility energizers to create descendants' luck. Indeed, the Chinese preoccupation with fertile marriages, and conjugal performance of the male has spawned all kinds of aphrodisiacs and symbols that supposedly create descendants' luck and reproductive performance. There are even different types of potions as well as supposedly 'auspicious times' to make love to ensure that any baby conceived is a male rather than a female child.

We can borrow from the list of recommendations given to young couples to ensure they have a happy love life. Here are some do's and don'ts that were passed to me by the older female members of my extended family.

Hanging a painting of children in a couple's bedroom is auspicious as it shows the happy result of their union.

- Decorate the bedroom in red during the early years of marriage. If red is found to be too strong use pink or peach. Red creates passion and a great deal of yang energy which brings good fortune to the union. White is a good colour for bedsheets, but do not use blue sheets. Blue carpets and wallpaper are fine.

- Never put live plants and flowers in the bedroom; but fruits are excellent, especially the pomegranate – a symbol of fertility.

- Paintings hung in the rooms of married couples should preferably feature children and ripe fruits signifying the happy result of their pairing. Flowers should be avoided. Once married, remove the painting of the peony since this only creates the danger of additional 'wives'. In the old days men could happily take on concubines. In today's world, the entrance of a sweet young thing into the marriage is not considered good feng shui. So better to keep the peony painting in the storeroom until your own daughters reach marriageable age and can benefit from its romantic fertility.

- Place small red lights to energize passion and fertility.

- Avoid anything that suggests water. Do not have an aquarium or basin in your bedroom. It causes misunderstandings and sleepless nights. A flask or glass of water is fine but not a painting of a lake!

- In the old days, wealthy families had the double happiness symbol carved in the form of elaborate designs into their bedroom furniture. You can also display this auspicious symbol in your bedroom, incorporating it into your bedroom design.

43

Get Help From Mother Earth

In feng shui when we speak of mother earth, we think of the whole practice itself. Feng shui refers to the luck of the earth and the earth element takes on significance because of this. Symbolically, the direction South-west and the trigram Kun (three broken lines) represent mother earth.

A feng shui master I met in Hong Kong once told me that there were three hexagrams in the I Ching that could be effectively harnessed to create different types of good fortune for the home. I had been advised that this gentleman was particularly well schooled in the I Ching and its interpretation for divinitive purposes, and that he was also knowledgeable about feng shui. He did not speak English, but I was fascinated by the way he explained the influence of each of the 64 hexagrams in the home. The three hexagrams he claimed could be effectively energized for the home were those known as Kun, Chien and Sheng.

For happiness in relationships and love and especially to foster family harmony he recommended that help be obtained from mother earth by displaying the hexagram Kun (which is created by doubling the three broken lines) in the South-west corner of the home. This, he said, would strengthen the energies of the mother of the family.

Above The trigram Kun rules the South-west and it symbolizes mother earth or big earth. It is considered to be the ultimate yin trigram and it personifies the female energy in everyone. You can draw on the energies of the Kun trigram to boost your love life.

Below
This mountain scene is one of the best representations of mother earth and symbolizes luck.

Chandeliers with all their hanging crystals create good yang energy. In your hallway, they can encourage chi into the home or if they are placed in the South-west they can bring luck in relationships.

Hang a Chandelier in the South-west

I am a great fan of chandeliers and use them lavishly to energize different types of good fortune chi in my own home. I hang a small one just outside my front door to seduce in the good chi, and I hang a slightly larger one in the foyer inside the main door to attract the chi to enter into my home. Then I place a really large one above my dining table to symbolize precious yang energy for the food on the table.

Create Harmony in the Home

But the most spectacular use of the chandelier is in the South-west of the home – where the combination of fire and earth brings wonderful love luck to every resident member. Married couples will be far happier with each other while younger members will never be short of boyfriends or girlfriends.

The chandelier in the South-west is an excellent activator of relationship luck. It makes everyone in the house popular with friends and family alike, and it also creates greater harmony within the home, thereby reducing friction between spouses and rivalry between siblings. Try to hang the chandelier in the South-west of the home, rather than the South-west of a single room.

45

Boost Social Life With Feng Shui

If you want to have a more active social life you need to light up your home's South-west corner. Here candles (fire) have been placed in water with petals (wood). By adding some pebbles (earth) and small metal pieces you would energize all the elements.

The best way to create the kind of luck that brings an active social life is to use bright lights to give a boost of yang energy to the South-west corner of your home. There are many ways to do this. The best method is to light up the South-west part of your garden with a very bright garden light. The placement of lights just outside the home, but within your domain attracts the precious mother energy of the South-west into the vicinity of your home.

Placing Bright Lights For Luck

The way I activate this aspect of my luck is to place three round lights on a pole placed about five feet above the ground. This is better than lighting from below. I also make sure that the rod holding the lights is hollow since this encourages earth energy to rise. Since the South-west is the place of big earth in terms of the five elements (see also Tip 11) this creates some excellent energy.

If you do not have a South-western part to your garden, or if you live in an apartment, it is a good idea to install a similar light if you have a balcony or terrace in the South-west. Those with roof gardens can also use the same method of activating the South-west part to the roof garden. If you like, you can also use two lamps instead of three since two is the number associated with the South-west.

If all you have to work with is a small apartment – a living room and a bedroom – then the thing to do is to energize the living room. Identify the South-west of your home with a compass. The corner, which is marked South-west on your compass, is the South-west. This corner is not determined by the location of your front door.

Place a standard lamp in that corner. Make it red, or a bright yellow or orange to strengthen the symbolism of yang energy. Such a lamp should not be so large as to dominate the room, but it should also not be too small. You can also place the lamp on a table. Whatever you do, the lights should be at least five feet above ground level. You can also hang a light in this corner. I hang crystal chandeliers in the South-west corners of all my public rooms, but do not do use this method in the bedroom!

Windchimes to Increase Your Popularity

There have been a great deal of contradictory recommendations regarding the use of windchimes as a feng shui-enhancing tool. It has even been suggested to me at several seminars of mine that hanging windchimes in the home could well attract wandering spirits who thus disturb the energies of the home. I want to say here categorically that windchimes are an excellent enhancing and positive tool. They do not attract 'spirits'. I have hung windchimes in my home for over 20 years and they have brought me nothing but good luck and good fortune. The key to creating auspicious energy by hanging windchimes is to consider these following three items.

- Are you are using windchimes made of wood, ceramic or metal? The material that your windchime is made of can enhance or destroy the element of the 'corner' in which it is placed. It is vital to get this right. To enhance the energies of corners use windchimes according to the element of the corner. This means metal chimes are best for the West, North-west, and North. Ceramic chimes are best for the South-west, North-east and centre. Wooden chimes are best for the East, South-east and South.
- Whether you are using windchimes to suppress the bad luck of a specific corner or structure or as a feng shui-energizing and enhancing tool. If you are using them to 'press down' the bad luck caused by an offensive structure or poison arrow, then you should use a metal windchime that has five rods.
- The number of rods you have in your windchime follows on my last point. As already mentioned, to enhance luck use six or eight rods. To suppress bad luck use five rods.

Windchimes can help to suppress bad luck or to enhance the energies in various corners of your home. The five metal rod windchime shown above is the best one to use to deflect a poison arrow.

To enhance your social popularity, hang either a two-or nine-rod windchime made of either crystal or ceramics in the South-west corner of your living room. This is a feng shui enhancing method best implemented in the public areas of your home. Do not apply this method in the bedroom or the study. To attract influential people into your life, select a windchime with six or eight rods made of metal and hang it in the North-western part of the living room.

47 Strengthen Friendships With Pine Branches

I have discovered that the use of pine branches to 'cleanse' homes of negative energy is used by certain Native American tribes of North America. In Tibet and Nepal, the dried leaves of pine trees are used to make pungent-smelling incense which I have been told is excellent for blessing abodes when used during prayer sessions, pujas or offerings to their deities.

In feng shui the pine tree is a popular and frequently used symbol of longevity, and is also associated with lifelong friendships. In the old days martial arts exponents who regarded themselves as blood brothers would seal their undying bond to each other by rubbing their palms with the smoke of a fire started with the twigs and dried leaves of a pine tree. The ritual involved rubbing the palms over the fire as the smoke rose and then rubbing each other's palm, before rubbing the face. This was believed to seal the

Pine trees are associated with a long life and friendship. So by placing a branch with three smaller branches in water by your front door you are encouraging these attributes into your home.

friendship until death. Any variety of pine tree is fine but the junipers are supposed to be the most potent for putting the seal on friendships.

Incoming Chi

If you want to use pine branches in feng shui, choose from varieties available locally. Christmas pines, junipers and any kind of cone shaped trees will do perfectly. Pluck a branch of pine. Then choose a branch which has three sub branches so that it symbolizes the three types of luck – heaven, earth and mankind luck. Then place the branch near the main door of your house. The foyer area is an excellent area, since this is where the incoming chi enters the home. For it to meet the auspicious symbol of pine leaves would be most beneficial.

Place the pine branch in water for a maximum of three days or until the pine needles start to drop. In addition to strengthening friendships, this will also create excellent long-life luck for the people who live in the house, and is especially recommended in homes occupied by older people. To strengthen the longevity luck of the father of the family, pine branches can be placed in the North-west corner of the living room. An alternative to using real pine leaves would be to hang a landscape painting of mountains filled with pine trees in the home instead.

Avoid Having Three in a Picture

Three in a picture is not recommended for friendships. However, three in a picture does no harm if the picture is of family members. Indeed, happy family portraits spell excellent feng shui (see Tip 30) and for those of you with three-member families (like me) the best feng shui method of taking pictures is to arrange yourselves in a triangle, placing the most important member of the trio at the apex of the triangle. This is illustrated in the two pictures below.

The Chinese are extremely superstitious about featuring three people in a picture. In fact, in the old days, artists were never allowed to paint three comrades in one picture. Even two people in a picture was deemed as unlucky. But three in a picture was believed to create the cause for conflict, or separation, between those shown in the picture. The feeling was that the one in the middle would be separated from the two people at the side. It is useful to keep this point in mind when snapping pictures with your friends.

Hanging Pictures in the Home

As for hanging pictures in the home here are guidelines to follow.

- Never hang photographs of family members directly facing a toilet.
- Never hang your picture directly facing an inauspicious direction (see the table in Tip 2 to check this).
- Never hang a family portrait directly facing the front door.
- Never hang a family portrait directly facing a staircase.
- Never hang family portraits in the basement.

Family Portraits

Three people pictured in a row is not recommended for friendships (above). But if your family only has three members it is considered to be beneficial if you photograph them in a triangle (right) with the most important member at the apex.

49

Seating Friends at a Dinner Party

Round tables are the most suitable for family eating and entertaining. For a harmonious evening, try and seat any guests according to their most auspicious directions.

If you want your dinner parties to be successful social occasions then, in addition to applying the generally accepted tips on entertaining, you might want to consider using some other feng shui techniques for making sure everyone has a good time. The feel-good factor can easily be put into practice by making certain that every guest is seated according to his/her most auspicious direction. Calculate their respective KUA numbers (See Tip 1) and find out their most auspicious directions. Then seat each of them according to at least one of their four excellent directions. Then there will be harmony and excellent rapport between everyone.

The practice of placing guests of different genders next to each other is excellent for ensuring good yin and yang balance, but this is not as important as getting their directions right.

Round tables are always to be preferred to rectangular tables, but rectangular tables are better than T-shaped or L-shaped arrangements. If the number of guests coming for dinner exceeds the number of chairs you have available, it is better to make it a buffet dinner rather than hastily adding chairs in order to have a sit-down dinner.

Your Seating Plan

There are some other important considerations.

● Never seat anyone at the corner edge of a square or rectangular table.
● Never seat anyone directly facing a toilet door.
● Never seat anyone directly facing the door into the dining room.
● Never seat anyone directly underneath an overhead beam.
● Never seat anyone directly facing a protruding corner.

Knives and Scissors in Friendships

When working at your desk, be careful never to leave scissors on the table with the pointed part facing you (or someone else). This transforms the harmless pair of scissors into a 'poison arrow' inadvertently pointing directly at you and sending hostile energies towards you. This same advice holds true for penknives, screwdrivers and other tools like hammers, drilling bits and so forth. Develop awareness for objects like these that lie around the home, and incorporate this awareness into your personal habits.

When you point a sharp object that is also hostile – like a knife or a pair of scissors – at a friend, you will create almost immediate friction between the two of you. Nothing kills friendships faster than the presence of a sharp object driving a wedge between you. Never give anything sharp as a present to anyone since the results are usually unpleasant.

Knives Make Horrible Gifts

A gift of anything that is sharp, pointed or hostile carries extremely negative energy and causes bad feng shui for the recipient of your gift. Chinese people never buy tools, knives and other sharp objects to be given as gifts. If you are inadvertently given something sharp as a present (such as a tool box, a handy Swiss knife or corkscrew opener for your wines) you can nullify the bad effects of the gift by immediately 'paying' for it with a token coin or note given to the present-giver. This symbolizes that you have 'bought' the gift yourself, thereby protecting yourself from the negative energy inherent in something so hostile being given to you. I recommend that this antidote be followed since the repercussions can sometimes be quite tragic. Do not dismiss this as superstition. Remember that superstitions are often the orally transmitted wisdom of our ancestors.

If you receive a sharp gift such as a Swiss army knife or a pair of sewing scissors, as shown, give the person a token coin to nullify the negative energies.

Create Good Luck For Those Around You

There is no better way of making and keeping the friends and neighbours in your life than to design your feng shui in a way that not only does not hurt them but, instead, enhances their sense of well-being. You should learn feng shui with the motivation of making certain that anything you build would not create bad feng shui for those who live around you.

By making certain you do not create bad feng shui for others, the energy that surrounds your environment will be filled with healthy chi that has not been defiled by the presence of negative 'poison arrows'. These can easily be created and caused inadvertently by your roof line, your house façade and your corner edges. It is for this reason that I am always reluctant to recommend the use of Pa Kua mirrors (see Tip 5) to solve simple feng shui problems. The Pa Kua mirror is a powerful tool, but it works by hurting others.

'Poison Arrows'

So when a 'poison arrow' is threatening my front door I prefer to use a windchime, or to plant plants that block out the 'poison arrow' rather than hang a Pa Kua which will definitely hurt my neighbour. If you keep this tip in mind, you will be adding to the creation of beautiful energy in your neighbourhood and benefiting everyone who lives around you.

You can also place lights along your borders to create excellent energies of good fortune for your neighbours. When placed near their front gate, this act of good neighbourliness creates harmony between you. If there is a fence between you and your neighbours, make sure they do not have designs that could hurt your neighbours. Sharp pointed arrows or triangles aimed at your neighbour's home causes ill fortune to befall them. It will rebound on you when your neighbour retaliates with Pa Kua mirrors. There will be no end to a feng shui war!

Getting on well with your neighbours and possibly socializing with them is always worthwhile, so avoid using Pa Kua mirrors as they can deflect negative energy towards them (left). You can also promote a harmonious relationship with neighbours by using rounded gate and fence designs that will not point poisonous arrows at their homes (above).

Pointing a Finger Creates Bad Feng Shui

It is wise never to allow anyone to point an index finger at you when they speak to you. This directs bad energy towards you. If you are subjected to too much finger pointing, you will definitely succumb to a large dose of bad luck. Likewise you should also refrain from pointing at someone when you speak to them.

In certain cultures it is regarded as extremely rude to point a finger as you speak. It puts people off you and the energies created will be most hostile. Advertisement campaigns or promotional literature which include such a gesture create very bad energy.

The most well-known advertisement of this sort was the American advertisement calling for recruits into the US army during the Vietnam War. 'Uncle Sam wants you' said the advertisement while a grouchy-faced man draped in the US flag pointed a finger directly at the reader. It was not a good advert from a feng shui point of view.

Never point a pair of scissors at anyone as you talk. It creates bad energy!

'Heaven Men' and 'Devil Men'

In feng shui, descriptions of helpful and unhelpful people are usually so colourful it is impossible not to be amused. However, when you receive help unexpectedly from an influential person, or when your career gets a huge boost due to a positive recommendation, then you begin to understand why feng shui describes such people as 'heaven men'.

Likewise, when you are the victim of a powerful person's vindictiveness, or when someone you trust betrays you, you will begin to understand why feng shui describes such people in your life as 'devil men'.

Your Chien Corner

Certain features in your feng shui can affect the presence or absence of helpful and unhelpful people in your life. This is mainly governed by the quality of the Chien corner of your home (or office). This is the North-west corner ruled by the trigram Chien – the ultimate yang trigram. Its corner in any home is vitally important and must be safeguarded at all times.

Your Chien Corner is not determined by your front door but by the compass direction of the North-west. Hang a metal windchime with eight hollow rods in your Chien corner to attract 'heaven men' into your life. By doing this you will also energize the luck of the family's father, which is doubly rewarding.

Do not place bright lights in the North-west corner of your home since this will attract 'devil men' into your life. The presence of the fire element in the North-west is extremely harmful. Make sure you do not place spotlights or chandeliers in this corner of your home or living room.

55 One For the Road – the Last Drink

A popular way to end a dinner party or evening is for the host to offer a last drink before the guests depart. When you are offered a last drink, feng shui advises that you should not refuse. Even if you take only a symbolic sip of water, this will make certain that you get home safely.

According to Chinese feng shui beliefs, the guest should never refuse the offer of a last drink or the last helping of food. To refuse generates the bad luck of travel. You could run up against obstacles on your journey home. Thus when you are a guest make certain you always take a small symbolic bite or sip of anything offered before you take your leave.

If you are offered a final drink at a dinner party, never refuse, even if you only drink water, as a refusal is supposed to generate bad luck for travelling.

56 The Feng Shui of Taking the Last Piece

Does taking the last piece of food at a meal or a party destine one to be a perennial bachelor or an unmarried old maid? Will it create obstacles for singles in search of a mate?

This is an old superstition that was passed down to me when I was in my teens. I was told that if I ate the last piece of chicken on the plate, accepted the last portion of cake, or generally always helped myself to a left-over morsel at the end of a meal, I would have a hard time landing a husband. So all through my teenage years I strenuously avoided being the person who took the last piece of food at any meal.

I did not discover the authenticity of this particular superstition until I discussed it with an old feng shui practitioner in Hong Kong who confirmed it. He told me that regularly taking the last morsel at any meal also created poverty energies and caused descendants' luck to become afflicted.

The Feng Shui of Serving Refreshments

When serving tea, coffee or drinks to your visitors make sure you do not point the spout of a tea-pot, coffee-pot or jug directly at anyone. These spouts are like tiny 'poison arrows' of hostile energy aimed at them.

When you are a guest, it is a good idea to lean over and move the teapot or jug, if the spout happens to be pointing directly at you. Otherwise, the spout is sending little slivers of 'killing breath' towards you. When entertaining, therefore, please be aware of this little point. 'Poison arrows' create small discords that can magnify into misunderstandings. I was told that in the China of the old days, Triads gangs often used the spout of the teapot as a secret signal to pinpoint adversaries to fellow members. Someone would lean over to reposition the teapot, so that the spout pointed directly at the 'outsider', sending secret 'poison arrows' his way.

When you are serving tea for your guests, try to make sure that you don't point the spout of the teapot directly at them as it can be harmful.

Never Serve with Chipped Crockery

Another piece of advice when entertaining friends is never to serve coffee or tea in a cup with a chipped rim, or serve drinks in a chipped glass. Drinking from a teacup or coffeecup which has even the smallest chip brings bad luck since this symbolically cuts the mouth, negatively affecting one's speech so that what you say will get you into trouble.

Crockery in the home should never be chipped or broken. It is a good idea to go through your crockery at home and to discard pieces of flawed porcelain. This makes sure you never use them either for yourself or for your guests.

The Chinese believe that drinking from chipped cups and glasses or eating from chipped bowls seriously affects one's 'rice bowl', which is another way of saying it causes one to suffer from bad luck in one's livelihood. If you are in business for yourself this rule becomes even more important since it affects your business. So be especially mindful with teacups.

Choosing Your Personal Work Space

If you want to enjoy good feng shui at work, you should try to select your work space carefully. Naturally, some people will have a greater say in where they may have their office than others, depending on their status. Nevertheless, you should do what you can to observe the following feng shui guidelines on choosing your personal work space.

Try to avoid sitting directly in front of a square pillar. The cutting edge of the pillar will create havoc in your work life. Success will be hard to come by, and you will get ill frequently. The best solution is to move out but, if you cannot, then you should try to deflect the bad energy with plants or with mirrors that are wrapped around the entire four sides of the pillar. This serves, symbolically, to make the column or pillar 'disappear'.

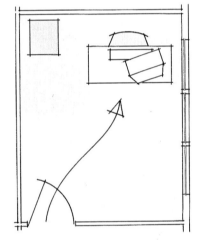

Desk Placement

The best place to have your desk in an office is in the far right corner, diagonally from the door (above).

Do not place your desk opposite the door in the office as this is not an auspicious position (right).

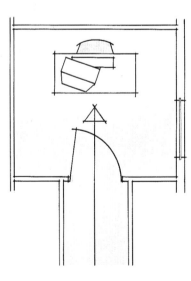

Guidelines

- Always try to have your office and desk in the far corner diagonal to the entrance door into the whole office. The deeper you are inside the office the better will be the feng shui.

- Never have your office or desk located at the end of a straight corridor or walkway.

- Do not sit in an office or desk that directly faces the entrance door.

- Do not sit in an office or at a desk that directly faces a toilet door or a staircase. Your chances for advancement will be severely curtailed.

- Do not sit in an office or at a desk that places you directly underneath an exposed overhead beam. You will suffer from endless pressure and headaches.

- Do not sit with your back to the door, whether it is the door into your private office, or the door into the main office itself.

- Never sit at a desk or place which subjects you to the cutting edge of a protruding corner. Move out of the line of fire and use a plant to block it.

Energizing Your Compass Group

G o to Tip 1 and check your four auspicious locations. From the table you will be able to determine if you are an East group or a West group person. The East group directions are East, North, South and South-east. The West group directions are West, South-west, North-west and North-east. Now follow the guidelines below to energize your group directions in your office.

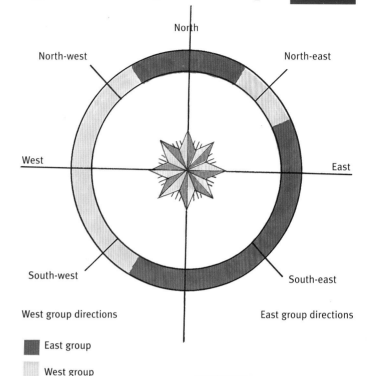

West group directions

East group directions

East group

West group

West Group Energizers
● Energize the West with a model aeroplane laden with coins tied with red thread. Bells and windchimes are also effective.

● Energize the North-west the same way. Do not put bright lights in either the West or the North-west as these will magnify all your problems.

● Energize the South-west with lots of natural crystals. If your main office door is also located in the South-west, then placing a large real crystal stone is most effective. A good friend of mine placed a large amethyst crystal boulder that had a deep 'pocket' to capture all the good fortune coming into the office. It brought him masses of business luck.

● Energize the North-east in the same way as the South-west but it is not necessary to display crystals that are too large.

Right
Putting a model of a terrapin (right) in a broad bowl of water can boost the North corner for an East group person.

Left
A piece of amethyst can help to energize the South-west corner for a West group person.

East Group Energizers
● Energize the East corner with plants, flowers and paintings that have lush vegetation and water. Avoid at all costs anything metallic in this corner. Windchimes, scissors and blades cause a lot of harm.

● Do the same for the South-east corner except here you can also display a miniature fountain, or a simple bowl of water.

● In the North, place a broad-based bowl of water with a terrapin inside. This can be real or fake. The real one is to be preferred.

● In the South, place something red – a painting, a red carpet, red cushions – and a bright light to energize the luck of a great reputation. Properly energized, the South brings excellent reputation luck.

Activating Your Lucky Directions

The correct application of the KUA formula directions in feng shui can be extremely potent (see Tip 1). This is not to be confused with the nine-star Ki formula used by some feng shui practitioners. The KUA formula is based on the two major symbols of feng shui practice – the Pa Kua and its eight trigrams arranged around the sides according to the later heaven arrangement and the nine-sector Lo Shu square.

To simplify the formula for readers, I have summarized the lucky and unlucky directions according to an individual's personal KUA number in Tip 2. But knowing one's auspicious directions is only half of the practice. To get the most out of this feng shui formula, the directions must be skilfully applied.

The best place to use the auspicious directions of one's KUA number is in the office. Check Tip 2 again to remind yourself of your lucky directions and then do at least one of these two things:

● Sit directly facing your sheng chi, i.e. your most auspicious direction, while working.
● Place your office in the location that corresponds to your sheng chi.

Avoid Your Unlucky Directions

It may not always be possible to sit in one's most favourable location, or face one's most auspicious direction, perhaps because of the presence of 'poison arrows'. If this is the situation, then it becomes a matter of great urgency to sit facing at least one of your three other auspicious directions. This is to ensure you do not succumb to the negative forces of your four unlucky directions.

Of your four lucky directions, the first is the best for career and business but it is the fourth that is the best for self-development.

You need to memorize your good and bad directions so that you can apply them in all situations. If your KUA number is 6, for example, your good directions are West, North-east, South-west and North-west. Your bad directions are South-east, East, North and South. Here in the top illustration the desk is facing North which is not a good direction for KUA number 6. However, in the bottom illustration the desk is facing West which is the best direction for number 6.

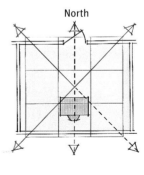

North

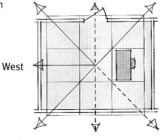

West

Protecting Against Bad Feng Shui

Bad feng shui in most offices is frequently traced to the entrance door being afflicted or 'hurt' by outside features.

- If the door that opens into your office is at the end of a corridor, it receives 'killing' chi (bad energy) every day.
- If the office door faces a bank of lifts or elevators, the constant opening and closing of the doors creates a great deal of imbalance.
- If the door faces a staircase, the chi is extremely negative and, if there are two staircases, one going up and the other going down, then there will be a great deal of disharmony and quarrelling in the office.

A cluttered desk is not good office feng shui as it will cause confusion and you could end up drowning in a sea of paperwork.

Features That Can Cause Bad Feng Shui in the Office:

- The sharp edge of a table
- A table piled high with files, excessive jumble creates too much yin.
- Open bookshelves resemble blades that send out killing energy (see also Tip 28).

Clutter

I have always maintained that keeping one's home and office clean and tidy is as much common sense as it is feng shui. Excessive disarray in the office, however, does cause confusion and therefore brings disharmony.

63 Avoiding Killing Chi

The 'killing breath' of the dragon inside any office is usually less lethal than that caused by the massive structures of the physical world outside. Nevertheless, sharp edges of furniture, cupboards, filing cabinets and the like often cause severe headaches, and office workers can succumb to tiredness and listlessness at best, and suffer from severe illnesses at worst.

Probably the most effective and aesthetic way of combating secret pointed arrows inside an office is to display large vases of flowers. Having said that, it is also important not to overdo things and turn your office into a flower shop!

When there are many square pillars inside an office – and this is usually the case in dealing rooms and newspaper offices, which have an open-plan arrangement – a solution must be found. In this situation, you can very effectively break up the killing chi by arranging fake silk trees that serve to soften the edges of pillars. Bringing fake trees into the office has another feng shui benefit as those trees symbolize growth – excellent for business. Of the five elements, wood, as symbolized by trees and plants is the best element to activate within the office. Fake trees are acceptable for feng shui purposes but they should be kept free of dust, and they should be regularly cleaned. They should not look sick and droopy.

So, in the office you should always be on the lookout for anything that is sharp, pointed, heavy and threatening-looking. Don't forget that many of these secret 'poison arrows' within your personal space are easily overlooked, unless you check for them.

64 Feng Shui 'Cures' For Sitting Problems

Develop the habit of looking around your personal space. Look up above you to check if you are sitting under an exposed overhead beam. These heavy overhead structures are very bad news and you really want to avoid them at all costs. Big exposed beams cause severe headaches, migraine, stress and a great deal of bad luck.

Look sideways to see if there are any pointed edges of walls, furniture and protruding corners that may be sending 'poison arrows' your way. Edges cut into you causing illness, stress, pressure and again, a great deal of bad luck. At work these pointed edges also create havoc with your career prospects. You cannot operate efficiently in such a situation so you should deal with such structures immediately, as soon as you become aware of their existence.

The best method of correcting these inauspicious features is to move your desk from under the beam, or away from the sharp edges. Hollow bamboo tied with red ribbon can also deflect the bad energy of overhead beams.

Slow Down the Energy in Your Space

Good harmonious shapes and auspicious lines

Bad sharp shapes and unlucky lines

When doing your feng shui in the office, just as in the house, always remember that anything sharp is harmful. It needs to be softened, blocked or put out of sight. Anything curved and softly flowing encourages the energy in the environment to slow down, settle, and be transformed into friendly energy.

Train Your Feng Shui Eye

Look at the shapes and lines drawn on this page. It is not difficult to train the eye to differentiate between what is potentially good and what is potentially bad feng shui. Thus art deco would tend to create harmful feng shui while art nouveau would create auspicious feng shui.

Anything that is straight will cause problems while anything circular brings good fortune. If you master these two simple rules of what is known as Form School feng shui you will be going a long way to train your feng shui 'eye'. When in doubt always select the option that allows the invisible energy lines in your personal space to slow down. Using plants, screens, curtains, and other soft furnishings allows you to achieve this result. When shapes are angular and threatening, either soften the edges or, if that is impossible, hang fabrics, use potted plants and, when all else fails, shine a bright light to counter the excessive sharp energy.

When selecting your particular feng shui 'cure' or balancing agent, be guided by the rules that govern the production and destruction of the five elements. Refer to Tip 10 for more on this. For example, in the fire corner you can energize a lack of fire energy with wood since wood produces fire. If there is already excessive fire energy caused by too many lights and too much red, use a water element, such as a blue carpet, to cool it down. When you practise feng shui in this way, you are going to the core of the practise and you will realize how easy it is and will soon be able to undertake feng shui diagnosis yourself.

66 Take Note of Seating Arrangements

Just as at home, in the office you should be careful not to sit facing the corner of a square table. If the sharp edge is pointed directly at you, harmful energy aimed straight at you will harm you. When there are five people seated at a small square table meant only for four, make sure you do not take the chair that is placed directly facing the corner edge of the table. Hostile energy will cause you to be unlucky for the rest of the day.

When attending an important interview, for a scholarship or a job, or when meeting your supervisor or your boss, you must endeavour never to sit facing the edge of the table. If you do, luck will be against you, and you are unlikely to be successful or get what you want. Always sit facing one of your four good directions (check back to Tip 2 to find out what these are).

Seating at Work

When you are involved in business meetings, always make sure that you do not sit with a pointed edge of a table facing you, as is happening to one of the men in this picture. If you do this you will have a poison arrow aimed at your stomach and will be placed at a disadvantage to the rest of your colleagues.

Orienting Your Negotiating Position

You can use feng shui to enhance your negotiating luck. Do this by simply sitting and facing one of your four auspicious directions. If the person you are negotiating with is sitting in his or her bad direction you will definitely have the edge. This holds true in any kind of interview or business negotiations. Discover your auspicious directions from the table in Tip 2.

If, once in a meeting, you cannot remember your auspicious directions, or you do not have a compass, do not attempt to guess your good direction. This will put you off course. Instead, use Form School feng shui instead by applying the following guidelines.

- Choose the seat that is furthest away from the door into the room.
- Never sit with your back to the door. In any negotiating scenario you must be able to 'see' the door. Otherwise you could get stabbed from behind, and also when you least expect it.
- Try not to sit with your back to the window, unless it faces a solid building. If you sit with your back to the window, in feng shui terms you are deemed to be sorely lacking in support.
- Avoid sitting directly underneath beams and ceiling designs that are sharp and heavy. Move your chair and swivel it around if necessary.
- Choose a chair that has an armrest and a high back. This provides the traditional feng shui support that allows you balance.
- Do not sit in a seat that forces you to have your feet pointed at the door as this is a

very inauspicious orientation.

- Finally, never sit with anything sharp or angular pointing directly at you. Move your chair away so that you can avoid being in the line of fire!

Always try and sit in one of your auspicious directions for a business meeting. If you can't take a compass direction, try to sit in one of the seats furthest from the door and never choose the seat with your back facing the door (above and left).

68

Energizing Your Desk Top For Career Success

Remember to always place your computer on the right of the desk, but place something higher on the left, such as a desk lamp as shown here.

Flowers

Place a vase of fresh flowers on the East side of your desk top. Do not allow flowers to overwhelm or block your view. Change the flowers as soon as the leaves turn yellow. Flowers create yang energy.

Plants

Place a very healthy small plant on the South-east corner of your desk top. This attracts a good income and enhances your chances of personal growth.

Crystals

Place a round crystal on the South-west corner of your desk top so that you create the luck of harmonious relationships with all your colleagues.

Lamps

Any kind of light energizes your good name and reputation when placed in the South. This is one of the most excellent methods of creating a solid reputation within your company, and your business community.

Calculators and Computers

All personal office equipment made of metal should be placed on a separate table that is preferably located on the West or North-west of your desk. If you need to have them on your desk top, place them on your right-hand side, but make certain you also have something higher to place on the left side. This ensures that the energies of the dragon prevail over the tiger.

Golden Rules

- You must be seated facing your sheng chi direction (see Tip 2).
- Leave the part of the desk directly in front of you empty of files, books and so on. Create a mini 'bright hall' or unencumbered space.
- Piles of files should be higher on the left than on the right.
- Place the phone in a corner that matches an auspicious personal direction for you.

Enhance Your Career

Feng shui is extremely potent when it comes to creating career luck. Indeed, during the old days when emperors reigned over China, the mandarins at court were especially mindful of ensuring good fortune. In those days of autocratic imperial rule, bad luck could well create the kind of misfortune that led to death, not merely for the official but also usually for his entire family. Career survival was thus a very serious matter. Feng shui was often applied to ensure protection from court intrigues.

In today's modern commercial and corporate environment, we have the equivalent of court intrigues in the form of 'office politics'. Feng shui can provide an excellent shield against being overwhelmed by internal politicking. It can safeguard you from being elbowed out of opportunities for advancement. And feng shui can also help to protect you from people who are jealous of your position or advancements. Thus you can both enhance and have protection in your career with feng shui.

Energize the North corner of your office. This is the universal corner associated with your good fortune at work. The ruling trigram of the North is the trigram Kan which means water. Feng shui water is respected as the bringer of great fortune. But water is also regarded as extremely dangerous when it breaks its banks. So you can tap the element of water for the North to create career luck but you must not overdo it. If you create too much water it will not be good and will drown you!

Place a small water feature, preferably with the water continuously moving, to signify movement and good yang energy in your North corner. A miniature water fountain that is about one foot in diameter would be the ideal feature to have!

Creating Support With a Mountain

In the office, never sit with your back to the door. Doing so invites deception and betrayal. You should always sit with your back supported. If your office is located on the top floor of a multi-storey building and you sit with your back to a window, the chances are that you will lack solid support in your work and career.

Sit with a painting of a mountain behind you but make sure it is big enough to be meaningful. Do not have mountain ranges that are too sharp since these fire element mountains are less useful. The best type of mountain for protection is a mountain that resembles the back of a turtle. If there is a view of mountain, then sit with your back protected by this mountain. Do not sit facing the mountain, even if it is your most auspicious sheng chi direction (see Tip 2) as, if you 'confront' a mountain, you will be overcome. In feng shui a form as large as a mountain almost always takes precedence over Compass School formulas.

A Turtle For Stunning Success

In feng shui folklore the turtle is regarded as a most auspicious and celestial creature which brings extreme good fortune. Everyone benefits from the symbolic presence of the turtle which is also a symbol of longevity. It is also the guardian of the North, which governs career luck! So hang a picture of a turtle in your office.

If you have a large enough office, one of the best feng shui tips I can pass on to you is to keep a single terrapin or tortoise in the North corner of your office. It is not necessary to keep more than one terrapin. The number of the North is 1, and a single terrapin or tortoise is more auspicious than a pair. This is an exception to the guideline for relationship enhancement where keeping mandarin ducks in a pair is considered more auspicious. In the case of the terrapin, what we are trying to do

is to activate the element as well as the celestial creature of the North to bring about excellent career luck. This tip is applicable even if the North direction is one of your bad directions under the KUA formula (see Tip 1). The symbolism of the terrapin transcends all Formula Schools of feng shui.

The terrapin is a reptile that likes both water and dry land. You can use an aquarium to keep your terrapin, or you can be as creative as you wish. Place a boulder in the container, and half fill it with water. Feed your terrapin fresh watercress or 'kangkong'. They love green vegetables. You can also feed them with terrapin food bought from a pet shop. There is no need to overfeed since they survive on very little. But it is important to change the water regularly. Remember to let the water stand for a little while to get rid of the chlorine in the water. Standing a pail of water in the sun for at least three hours before using it for the terrapin gives it yang-energized water.

Terrapins are believed to bring wonderful luck to the owner. So if you can, keep one in the North corner of your office.

A Water Symbol For Good Fortune

If you can find a beautiful painting of water to hang in front of you in the office, and if the wall facing you is either North, East or South-east, it will bring exceptionally good fortune into your work life.

If the wall that faces you is not one of these directions, this tip is not for you. Remember that water is a double-edged tool. It can be very potent, but only when used correctly.

A view of water without mountains is better than a view of water with mountains. If the mountain is far way, the picture is acceptable. If the mountain is too much in the foreground, it can represent obstacles in your work in spite of the water. If you use water symbols, make them small so they do not seem to overwhelm you.

A picture or painting of a sailing boat, loaded with wealth and sailing towards you, is also a most excellent symbol for good fortune.

Auspicious Pictures

An inspiring picture or painting of a scene with water which is hung in front of you in the office can give you success in your business life. If mountains are in the picture, as shown here, make sure they are in the background. The sailing ship in the foreground is also a symbol of good fortune.

73

Position Your Telephone For Luck

If you want to feng shui the telephone and fax machine in your office, you must first observe from what direction the energy that brings the messages through the phone line is coming. This is considered the source of the telephone's energy.

The next thing to do is to position the phone so that the source of messages, calls and so forth is coming from your most auspicious direction – your sheng chi direction (see the table in Tip 2). Do not make the mistake of thinking it is the wall plug we are talking about. It is where the connection lead itself is plugged into the phone that matters. Good news and opportunities will flow your way if this is correctly positioned.

If your sheng chi is East then you should place your phone in such a way that the incoming wire enters the phone from the East. If your sheng chi direction is impossible to tap you should try to use one of your other three auspicious directions using the table in Tip 2 to check these).

The application of this feng shui method is a modern interpretation of an ancient formula ensuring that energy comes to you from your most favourable direction. This is equally applicable in all aspects of your working and family life. Always remember, however, that it is the source of energy that is important, so make sure you get this right.

Phone/Fax Placement

Placing your fax in your sheng chi direction (right) will help to make all the messages that come from that direction auspicious ones.

When positioning your phone (right) make sure you place the plug at the back in your good direction, not the one at the wall.

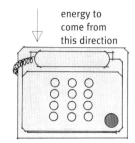

energy to come from this direction

energy coming from here

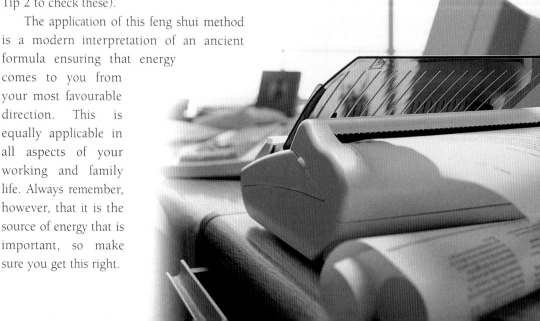

Place a Lucky Crimson Bird in the South

The South is the abode of the crimson phoenix which symbolizes strength in adversity. The phoenix also brings the luck of opportunities. When you energize this king of all feathered creatures, you are also activating the beneficial energies of the South. The luck of this particular sector suggests a great brightness because the South is also the place of the element of fire. Thus a crimson feathered creature to symbolize the phoenix is extremely auspicious.

Since it is really quite difficult to find a suitable picture or sculpture of the legendary phoenix, you can use any kind of beautiful bird that has colourful (and preferably red) plumage to represent the beneficial presence of the phoenix. The swan, the rooster, the peacock, and even the longevity birds – the crane and the flamingo – are all suitable.

A Symbol of Success

There are stunning bird sculptures made of ceramics and crystal that you can purchase to display in the South corner – either on a table or inside a cabinet. The effect is most auspicious. Not only will your reputation be enhanced over the years, but you will achieve recognition and attain great success in your chosen profession.

If you can obtain a piece depicting the crimson phoenix itself that would be even better. During my days at the helm of my department store in Hong Kong, I displayed a stunning gold-embedded crystal phoenix in the South corner of my office to reflect my goal of giving my department store a successful new image. The feng shui of the phoenix

This emblem of the phoenix in flight (right) will bring in beneficial energies to the office if it is placed in the South corner. Other paintings or sculptures of beautiful birds such as the flamingo or parrot (above) can also be used in this area.

worked beautifully and my store prospered!

A picture of an eagle in full flight is also an excellent symbol of success. In addition to representing the winged creature of the South, the eagle is also associated with strength, power and authority. Show an eagle flying or perched on a tree. Do not show an eagle looking fierce and predatory.

The Number 8 and Other Lucky Numbers

Numbers have feng shui implications for career and business success. There are individual lucky and unlucky numbers, and Chinese businessmen are most particular about the numbers of their telephones, their addresses, their car numbers and their bank accounts. They will never let the critical numbers of their commercial life to have what they deem to be unlucky numbers.

Eight is considered to be one of the luckiest numbers by the Chinese, and many try to have it included on their car number plates.

The Number 8 For Prosperity

The number 8 is widely regarded by Chinese as a universally lucky number. The feng shui explanation given is that phonetically it sounds like 'growth with prosperity'. (Much of feng shui symbolism is based on the sound of the symbol used.) There are tycoons in Hong Kong who happily part with a cool million dollars for the privilege of having the single number 8 on their car number plates.

In telephone numbers, credit cards and bank accounts, the Chinese also like to end their numbers with the letter 8 as they believe that this brings good fortune to their financial accounts. When the number is prefixed with 6, 7, 8 or 9 the luck is regarded to have doubled.

Lucky Numbers

In addition to the number 8, other lucky numbers are 1, 6 and 9. Prefixed with a 4 these numbers become even luckier. The number 9 is especially superior since 9, multiplied by any number of times, and then reduced to a single number always becomes 9 again. Nine represents the fullness of heaven and earth. Another lucky number is 7 because we are currently, until 2003, in the period of 7 according to the Chinese calendar. The number 13 is not considered an unlucky number whereas the number 14 is.

Unlucky Numbers

The most unlucky number, according to the Chinese, is the number 4 because the word for it sounds like 'death' in many dialects. Thus any series of numbers that ends with a 4 is a major taboo. The unlucky numbers based on Flying Star feng shui are the numbers 5 and 2 and also the numbers 2 and 3 together. However, some people regard 2 as a good number that means easy.

Block Out Excessive Sunlight

While it is excellent to energize your desk top and the corners of your office, it is also important not to forget about the balance of yin and yang energies in the office. Generally speaking, the presence of precious yang energy is very important and beneficial in an office environment.

However, when there is too much yang energy, the effect can be catastrophic. Excessive yang energy often comes in the form of strong sunlight caused by an office that has a west-facing wall. The brightness and heat of the afternoon sun, especially during the summer months, can create an excess of fire energy. Such a situation will create disharmony in the office. Flared tempers and impatience will be the order of the day. You must do something about it if your office falls into this category.

Block With Curtains

Use fairly heavy drape curtains to block out the afternoon sun completely. If you live in the Tropics like I do, the afternoon sun can be so glaring and hot that it completely dissipates my energy. The most effective way of combating this excessive yang energy of the sun is to use the water element. So curtains should be blue to simulate the water element. White curtains are also very effective since the West is the place of metal and white is symbolic of metal. Although fire burns metal, and thus can overcome white, if you use thick drapes the sunlight will be kept out. You will find after doing this that the yang energy comes under control and people will be less quarrelsome.

Dissipate by Hanging Cut Crystals

Another method of controlling excessive sunlight is to hang balls of cut crystal to catch the sunlight. This also creates wonderful rainbows inside the office by breaking up the light into colours.

This method seeks to harness the good energies of the sun and is best used in countries where the sun is not too hot. In the Tropics, unless the sunlight is kept out with curtains, drapes and shutters, the glare will turn the energy hostile despite the presence of the crystals and the rainbow sunlight.

If you work in a sunny office you will need to shield out the sun as it can create upset and disharmony. Blinds or heavy curtains will be very effective.

77 Use Colours For Good Fortune

Black

In feng shui, black represents water and white represents gold or metal. Although neither colour is preferred over the other, it is important to note that, generally, black should never be used for ceilings and roofs. I once saw a black ceiling, that instantly reminded me of a overhanging cloud, in a furniture shop. The feng shui was bad, and the shop closed after six months. Black above always spells danger. In your office I would strongly recommend that you avoid large patches of black. Don't use black on the walls, ceilings and carpets.

White

On the walls and ceilings use white instead. Apart from being a very yang colour (as opposed to black being very yin) white's symbolism is prosperity. Although white is also considered a mourning colour this is not the bright pure white. Mourning white is like sack cloth and is regarded as off-white – a yin

This black and white endless knot is an auspicious symbol. You can include it as a pattern or motif in your office decor, or frame it for good luck.

Pure white is a good colour to use for the walls and ceiling of your office. Then you can add red, green and blue in the appropriate compass directions.

colour. The bright white I refer to is a yang colour and I highly recommend it.

Red

This is the colour of the South, and shades of this colour on your south wall could well bring you good fortune. I recommend that if you want to energize the red family of colours, go for a warm peachy shade of red and use it in the South and also in the West symbolically to 'tame the tiger of the west'. You can apply feng shui colour therapy to your wallpaper, your curtains and your carpets – in fact all your soft furnishings in the office.

Green

This is the colour of money especially when activated and given prominence in the South-east. It is also very applicable for the East. Combine various shades of green if you wish, but always remember that a bright green that symbolizes the growth of spring is what you want to energize. Use fake silk trees with bright happy green leaves to energize better income luck for your office.

Blue

This is the colour of water. You can use it to good effect in the East, the South-east and North corners of your office space. Never overdo on the blue since water should never be activated in large quantities.

Feng Shui Dimensions For Chairs and Tables

The year I ordered a new desk made to feng shui dimensions, I was promoted so many times it became embarrassing. I was appointed the first woman CEO of a publicly listed company in Malaysia. It was also the year I became the first woman in Asia to head a bank. Today, the desk I use to write my bestsellers is exactly the same dimensions. I share the secret with you and wish you loads of luck.

Chairs

The chair you sit on at work should have a high back to symbolize back support. Chairs that do not completely cover your back represent poor feng shui. The chair shown in the illustration could thus be improved if the back were a little higher.

Your chair should also have armrests . Chairs without armrests have the dragon and tiger missing. Once again that spells bad feng shui. Use a height of 109 cm (43 in) for your chair back. This brings prosperity luck.

A Perfect Desk

Ideally your office desk should be made to feng shui dimensions (see right and below). Try to use a chair with a high back and arms so that you have the support of the dragon and tiger.

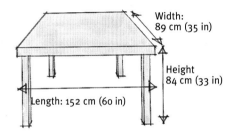

Width: 89 cm (35 in)

Height 84 cm (33 in)

Length: 152 cm (60 in)

79 Networking Luck From the North-west

Decorative feng shui is based on an understanding of the concept of *wu xing* or the five elements and, according to this, the North-west is the place of big metal. So this is the corner where all the gold and symbolic wealth of the office should be kept. The safe can definitely be kept here. In your own personal office, place your most important piece of metallic furniture here – it can be your safe, or your computer or even your photocopying machine.

The North-west corners of your workspace and office have the greatest impact on your helpful people and networking luck. When the North-west is correctly energized and the yin/yang balance is scrupulously maintained, you will find all your plans and ambitions succeed really easily. You will find that most people you do business with, or with whom you have to interact with, are always prepared to help you.

Use a compass to determine the North-west corner in your office. If you superimpose the Lo Shu or Pa Kua (see Tip 16) over your office layout plan as shown you can determine the North-west corner as soon as you get your bearings.

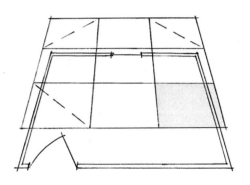

By putting the Lo Shu or Pa Kua square over your workspace you can work out your North-west corner. When you energize this area you will find that your business ambitions are achieved much more easily.

80 Use a 'Wealth Bucket' For Prosperity

A 'wealth bucket' filled with coins is a wonderful way of reflecting and magnifying the metallic energies of the North-west. Use a decorative container made of metal and, after filling it with coins, place it inside a cabinet in the North-west. Do not display this openly.

You could also place a bogus gold ingot in the North-west to simulate the essence of gold. The Chinese display lots of this fake gold during the lunar New Year in the hope that the symbolic placement will simulate the real thing. Decorative feng shui is very symbolic, and it is for this reason that during the New Year, an incredible number of auspicious symbolic objects are used to decorate the home.

Boost your North-west office corner with imitation gold ingots to mirror its metallic energies.

Plants in the South-east For Profits Luck

For as long as I have worked, I have always placed a foliage of bushy plants in my office. During my pre-feng shui knowledge days, I displayed plants because I always felt better when I had a plant inside my room. Today I do it because I have experienced the powerful effect which plants have on one's feng shui.

They are especially potent when placed in the South-east corner of the office. Irrespective of whether you're a West or an East group person (see Tip 1), everyone can activate the wonderful wealth energies of the South-east. This is the corner characterized by small wood, which is more valuable than big wood. Small wood is best symbolized by plants and by the colour green.

Choosing Auspicious Plants

Fake plants are completely acceptable and they are better than the dried plants that seem to be so popular with florists' shops. Choose ficus plants that have broad, rounded leaves. The money plant with its jade-like succulent leaves is another excellent choice.

Avoid plants that have thorns. Cactus plants are a major taboo. I have seen friends of mine suffer from the most severe bad luck simply because they placed cute little cactus plants on their windowsill. Cactus sends out little slivers of bad energy which, when accumulated over a period of time, causes misfortunes. When my friends removed their cactus plants, their problems were soon solved and their well-being improved noticeably.

Displaying the symbol of the oak (above), preferably with acorns, in your South-east office corner is said to bring success and prosperity.

Always avoid having cactus plants in the office as their thorns are thought to send out bad energy. They are best cultivated outside in gardens (right).

82

Coins and Bells For Prosperity

Hanging some bells, threaded with red ribbon, on the outside doorknob of your office door can attract good fortune.

When you use coins and bells for feng shui purposes, you should always tie them together with red thread or red ribbon since this energizes the essence of their symbolic meanings. You can use ordinary copper coins but it is best to use the old Chinese coins that have a square hole in the centre.

Coins on the Inside

Coins tied together with red string should be placed on the inside of the door. This symbolizes that prosperity has already entered your office. If you place coins on the outside of the door, it denotes only a state of eventual prosperity, the promise of prosperity which could well not materialize. It is not necessary to display a hundred coins! In feng shui more coins do not necessarily translate into a larger quantity of wealth luck. Three coins is sufficient. Do not place five coins as it is not a number conducive to wealth creation.

Bells on the Outside

If you hang some bells just outside your door, on the doorknob, it attracts good fortune chi (or energy) to enter your office. Symbolically the sound of bells announces the coming of prosperity and good news. Placing bells outside the office door, especially if your company, or the company you work for, is engaged in the trading, wholesale or retail business is an excellent feng shui feature.

Again do not overdo things. Choose small bells made of metal if the main door is facing West, North-west, or North. Do not use metal bells in the East and South-east. Here, use ceramic or crystal bells. The same goes for the South, South-west and North-east. This creates more harmonious element energies and is thus more auspicious.

Create Element Harmony in Door Design

Door designs can be made to harmonize perfectly with the direction they face, which often corresponds with their location in the office or house layout. If your main door faces the East or South-east then Door A illustrated below would be ideal since the rectangular design on the door indicates the growth element of wood, which in turn is the element of the East and South-east. This design is also suitable for the South since wood produces fire in the productive cycle (see Tip 10).

Your Ideal Door

If your main door is located in, or directly facing, the West and North-west, a door design that represents the metal element is auspicious. An example of this is shown as Door D. Circular designs and shapes belongs to the metal element which is the reason

moongates are often a feature along the West side of the garden of many old Chinese family homes.

The water design or a shape which is wavy is excellent for the North, itself a corner that symbolizes water. Water patterns are also excellent for doors that face East and South-east. An example of a water design door is shown as Door C.

The fire design door is perfect for doors that face South. The triangular pointed design (shown as Door E) is also excellent as a defensive type of door design that effectively blocks any bad energy that may be coming towards the office. The fire design door is doubly excellent for people born in a fire year.

Finally the square earth design (Door B) is ideal for North-east and South-west.

Doors to Suit the Elements

A

B

C
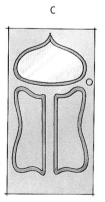

D

E
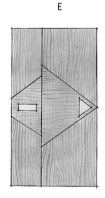

door with wood element   door with earth element   door with water element   door with metal element   door with fire element

The Luck Implication of Windows

Although windows are less important than doors in feng shui, it is helpful to know about the luck implications in window design. This has to do with which shape represents the different elements and the colour, as well as where and how many windows there are. The windows in your office are places where the energy of the room enters and leaves although they are secondary to the doors. Nevertheless, windows that have good views and are designed to balance with spatial feng shui concepts bring greater harmony to the workplace than windows that have not been planned in accordance to feng shui.

According to feng shui recommendations office windows should open outwards to symbolize a welcoming gesture to the good energy that floats in the outside environment. Feng shui stays silent on windows that slide open up or down. This point can thus be ignored. The most important thing about the window is that it should not, at any time, undermine the luck of your office. The following guidelines about windows should be useful.

This office has windows on every wall which is not good feng shui as it could cause loss of wealth to the business.

- There should not be too many windows. A ratio of three windows to every one door is about sufficient.
- Windows should not occupy every wall in a room. The best configuration is that only two walls should have windows. When there are too many windows it represents loss of wealth, and loss of income.
- Windows should not be directly opposite the main door. Chi flies in and flies out again just as quickly. The effect is like having a mirror directly facing the front door and that is also inauspicious.
- Use element shapes to create harmony between the windows of your office and that of the five elements present in your personal space.

Keep the Feng Shui Fish For Good Fortune

The Chinese of Malaysia, Singapore, Thailand and Indonesia are familiar with the magical qualities of the arowana. They refer to this freshwater tropical fish as the feng shui fish, and business tycoons pay thousands for a full-grown specimen. The scales of this fish are silver and they shimmer in shades of pink as an omen of good fortune. Arowanas are available in the UK and Europe. The fish grow to a length of about three feet.

My Personal Experience

In 1987, I installed a large aquarium in the living room of my apartment on the Peak in Hong Kong. I knew I would have to restructure my life if I were to be able to spend enough time with my daughter Jennifer. And I also knew that to stop working I had to make enough money to retire. I turned to feng shui and bought five

Arowanas are thought to be lucky fish. Feed them river worms or goldfish to bring out their auspicious pink scales.

arowanas from a Hong Kong pet shop. I fed my arowanas a diet of live goldfish to bring out the pink glow. My arowanas' scales glimmered in a range of red, gold and pink colours! They were truly beautiful.

In eighteen months they grew from 25 cm (10 in) to 46 cm (18 in). In that same time I also succeeded in my game plan. I had made enough to stop working and to return home to Malaysia.

I was offered $300,000 Hong Kong dollars for my arowanas but, instead, released them into the local reservoir. Each fish circled three times in front of me before swimming off into the depths of the water!

How to Keep Arowanas

Businessmen who keep these fish in the office usually have a huge aquarium that has nothing but water and a single arowana. There is no need to decorate the aquarium with water plants and sand. The arowana eats anything in sight. If you keep this fish, feed it fresh river worms or small goldfish to bring out the valuable pink glow. If you use specially packed fish food, get the best. Unless your arowana looks good it will not bring you wealth luck. Keep it either in the North, East or South-east of your office. It is not necessary to have an oversize tank!

86

Hang Auspicious Art in the Office

I have seen the most won-
derful feng shui art
hanging in corporate offices
and I have also seen some
horrendous examples. Here
are some feng shui ground
rules on what type of art to
have in the office.

Paintings of fish, such as the one on the right of carp, can bring good energies into the office environment.

- Generally avoid abstract art
  that has too many sharp
  edges and colours that
  clash with the elements on
  the wall where they are
  hung. Art that suggests
  metal could be harmful
  when hung on the East or
  South-east (see Tip 10).

- Also avoid pictures that
  show wizened old men or
  art that records the
  tragedies of our age. These
  can set up negative vibrations that can
  translate into bad luck. If you want to hang
  portraits of the monarch, or the founder of
  your company the best corner is the North-
  west wall. Hung here, the painting becomes
  transformed into a potent feng shui tool and
  it activates the luck of the magnificent
  trigram Chien.

- The best art to have in the office is landscape art. Feng shui is about the landscape,
  and if you can bring it into the office in a
  way that does not create imbalance, you will
  enjoy harmonious feng shui. A good rule of
  thumb is to place a mountain painting
  behind you and have a water feature in

front of you. A carpet of flowers in a field in
front of you is also excellent as this symbolizes a 'bright hall' of unencumbered space
in front of you.

- Paintings of flowers and fruits are also good
  feng shui, but it is not a good idea to hang
  peonies and other flowers that signify
  romance. Hang paintings of fruits on walls
  on the East side.

- Paintings of fish can often bring about wonderful feng shui energies but be very wary
  of using paintings of wild animals.
  Depictions of these magnificent cats – the
  tiger, leopard, and the lion – can sometimes
  cause problems.

Keep Your Office Secure

If you are neurotic about security, a popular feng shui method of keeping unwanted visitors and troublemakers out of your office is to place a broom upside-down just outside your entrance door each time the office is kept locked – in the evenings and during the weekends. Do not leave your broom there during working hours since the broom will sweep all your business visitors away. So, do not forget to remove the broom each morning when you come to work.

Keep unwanted visitors from your office out of working hours by leaving an upturned broom outside the door.

Hide Cleaning Equipment

All cleaning equipment – brooms and dust pans – is deemed to symbolize bad luck, and must be kept out of sight of the entire office, and especially the main door. The connotation here is that the presence of the broom in the vicinity of the foyer area sweeps out all your good fortune. Brooms are thus regarded as anathema to feng shui. Keep them inside cleaning cupboards or storerooms. Likewise the waste bin should be kept out of sight too and preferably covered. Place your wastepaper basket under your table where it is not visible from the main door, or the door into your private office (if you have one).

Wastepaper bins are believed to take away good fortune, so should be kept out of sight.

89

Activating Your Career Luck

If you are seriously amb-itious to make it big in your career, you can use feng shui to give yourself a boost. Good career feng shui usually manifests itself in the form of increased opportuni-ties. It will make you a much busier person so, unless you are prepared to grab new opportunities that come your way, the benefits will be limited. It is important to realize this, otherwise you could well feel hassled by the sudden new opportunities available to you. Those of you who are workaholics, however, will benefit tremen-dously when you activate

Quick Tip
If your career corner is in your bathroom you can try putting some big boulders in there to push down the bad energy caused by the toilet.

your career luck. Your hard work will start to reap dividends. Powerful bosses will notice you within your work place, and extra responsibilities will be heaped upon your shoulders. You will start to operate in a different league.

When I energized my career luck, it took off so fast I did not know if I was coming or going. That was in the year 1982, a year I made so many quantum leaps in my career it scared me. So when you start energizing your career luck be prepared to be surprised.

Energize the North

The career corner is the North of any residen-tial building or personal space. Thus, to get the most out of career feng shui you should

use feng shui methods to energize the North corner of both your home and your office.

At home, if the North corner is your bedroom, do not do anything inside the bedroom. Instead, you can activate the North corner of your living room. If the North corner is where you have the toilet, the conse-quences are inauspicious for the careers of people who live in the house. Close the toilet and, if you can, try not to use it. The way to overcome the negative effect of the toilet is to place a big boulder inside the room to press down on the bad chi (or energy) caused by the toilet.

To create good yang energy, in the North of your living room and your office, place an aquarium full of lively guppies.

Success Luck With Feng Shui Doors

Career luck is much improved when the location, direction and design of the door that leads into your private office is planned according to feng shui principles. It is not possible to get everything correct but you should always endeavour to observe some of the major taboos.

- Start by making sure your door is not being hit by anything harmful. These are sharp edges, long corridors, exposed beams, corners and pillars.
- Next try to have your door located in a corner of your room, and facing a direction that is auspicious to you. If your door cannot face your best direction, at least make sure it is not facing your chueh ming or total loss direction. This is regarded as a major feature to observe. (Check back to Tips 1 and 2).
- Avoid putting glass panels on your door. Transparent glass is more harmful than opaque glass, but both are to be avoided. Select door designs that are harmonious with the element of the corner in which it is located (see Tip 10) and, if you like, you can even

Good Feng Shui Doors

- Try to avoid having sliding doors opening into your office, or into your study at home. Doors should always open inwards to be auspicious.
- Doors should be solid and firm to be auspicious. Doors should also be large enough to comfortably accommodate the occupant of the room.
- When planning your office, put your door in one of your auspicious directions. A solid door that opens inwards is best as ones with glass panels or sliding doors are not to be recommended. Match the design of the door to its directional element and if it is to be painted choose the right colour for the element.

Below
Your office door should be solid, open inwards, and not have glass panels as this one below.

paint your door according to the next point.
- Door colours to aim for are brown for East and South-east; white for West and North-west; maroon for South; black for North; and beige for South-west and North-east.

91

Sitting in Your Power Position

The power position in any office is the corner that is diagonally opposite the main door. It is deep inside the office. Try to place your desk in this spot to get the most career luck. The following positions are best.

● Sit facing the door. Never have your back to the door as this will mean you losing out in any office politicking. It also means anyone working for you will betray you, and you will have a hard time managing them.
● Sit with a solid wall behind you. Do not have the window behind you.
● Sit with more space in front of you than behind you. If possible have a minimum of three feet of space in front of you.
● Sit with windows to your left or in front.

To activate the North (or career) corner of your house or office it is important to take your directions correctly. The North, (or any corner) of a body of enclosed space is where the compass needle points to. In feng shui we speak of the magnetic North as opposed to the true North. So invest in a good compass and, then, standing in approximately the centre of your office, note where the needle points to. To demarcate the North (and other sectors) of your office, divide your office floor area into nine equal grids. It is then a simple enough matter to identify exactly where your North sector is situated.

Good Seating Position
The most powerful position to sit in is in the corner diagonally opposite the main door of your office. This is the best area for success in your career.

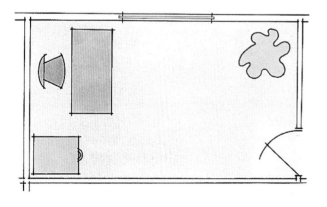

Desk Shapes and Placement

Place a regular rectangular-shaped desk diagonally opposite the entrance door of your office. Position your sitting direction according to your good directions (see the table in Tip 2), but make sure you face the door. If there is a beam above, move the desk out of its way. Do not have an L-shaped, or a U-shaped table as these are considered inauspicious from a feng shui viewpoint.

Desks are usually made of wood and this is excellent. Some business tycoons I know opt for glass-topped office desks and these are acceptable as long as they are West group people. If they are East group people glass tops are unsuitable. (See the table in Tip 1 to check your group.)

Elaborately carved desks are very auspicious. Chinese rosewood desks that have dragon carvings are believed to be especially auspicious. If you can afford a such table, I strongly recommend it since it will create wonderful success and prosperity symbolism. Mother-of-pearl inlaid desks are also extremely auspicious.

Auspicious Desks
U-shaped and L-shaped desks are considered inauspicious from the feng shui point of view. It is better just to sit at one rectangular-shaped desk, or even better a desk that is decorated with carvings of auspicious symbols such as dragons and other lucky creatures as they attract good fortune at work.

93

Find Your Best Directions For Business Travel

Look at the map of the world here. When planning your business trips note the direction of your travel. See what direction you are travelling from and travelling to! Now you need to use your KUA number to determine your travel feng shui. Go to Tips 1 and 2 and note your best and worst directions according to the Compass School formula. The rule to note is that you will get excellent feng shui luck in your travel and business trips if you travel from one of your best directions. Please note that it is the direction you travel *from* that is important, not the direction you are travelling to. Many people have got this interpretation wrong; even my feng shui master himself got it wrong for many years until he checked the classical old text again.

When you are going on business trips around the world, work out whether it is a favourable direction for you by using your KUA number.

Planning Your Business Trips Carefully

If you are an East-group person, then you know that travelling towards the West is generally favourable since then you are flying from the East, thereby bringing good luck with you wherever you are going. If you are a West-group person, then the opposite holds true. You are better off travelling towards the East.

If you live in the UK and you are an East-group person, and you have to make a business trip to Hong Kong, you will not be flying with feng shui luck since you would be flying from the direction North-west which is one of your inauspicious directions. This travel direction is suitable for a West-group person. For those making the journey the other way, i.e. from Hong Kong to the UK, the travel direction is South-east, which is suitable for an East-group person.

This aspect of feng shui practice is also applicable for travel within a country or within a city. If you travel to work every day from a direction that is auspicious for you, it is better for you, so check out your feng shui route.

Win Recognition With Feng Shui

There is no greater boost to your career than for your efforts, skill and expertise to be acknowledged and recognized by someone in authority. Luck has often been described as 'being in the right place at the right time'. So, if you have luck, you will surely catch the eye of someone who is in a position to enlarge your responsibilities and further your career.

Feng shui works wonders in enhancing this type of luck. Throughout my career days, every piece of work I did often got recognized and acknowledged, so that my climb up the career ladder was peppered with gratifying instances of recognition. Those were heady days indeed.

So let me share a career tip on getting recognized. Remember it is not enough to be hardworking and clever. Almost everyone has some skills to speak of and many people work very hard yet never get recognized. You must be perceived as success material. Only then will your skills be translated into promotions, higher income, more responsibilities and so forth. This requires luck, and feng shui can often provide this kind of luck.

Using a Crystal

All through my working life I placed a very large rectangular cut crystal made by Tiffany's on my desktop. I chose a rectangular shape because this represents the wood element that was beneficial for me. It was also in harmony with the celestial dragon of the East, whose element is also wood.

I placed this crystal on the left-hand side of my desk and often used it as a paperweight. The combined energies created by the intrinsic earth essence of the crystal and by the wood element that represented growth were most beneficial. You can do the same.

Helpful Crystals

Placing an ornament which contains the clear quartz crystal (right) on your desk can help to energize your career. Ideally use one which matches the shape of your beneficial element.

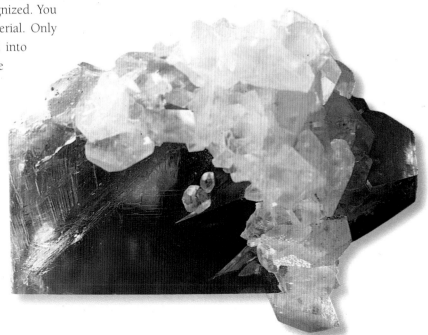

95

Energizing the Feng Shui of Your Files

It is not necessary to energize all your files – only the important ones that contain letters and documents connected with your work and your business. I energize all my files as well as my investment files. This helps to create prosperity energies for the success of my work and, to date, this method has not failed me.

You will need Chinese coins with a square hole in the centre. Take three of these coins and tie them together, yang side up, either with a red ribbon or with red thread. (The yang side is the side that has four instead of two characters.) Tape the coins onto the covers of your files with strong cellophane tape, checking occasionally to make sure that the coins do not fall off.

Protecting the Feng Shui of Your Files

- Never allow your important files to be stepped upon. You should never place them on the floor no matter how busy you are or how cluttered your office gets. When your files get stepped upon it creates extremely negative energy that affects your work luck.
- Never allow your important files to be placed under the table either. This also has the same bad effect.
- Never place any important files under staircases. This also means that filing cabinets must not be under staircases.
- Never place files next to a toilet. And filing cabinets should not be placed against a wall which has a toilet on the other side.

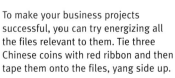

To make your business projects successful, you can try energizing all the files relevant to them. Tie three Chinese coins with red ribbon and then tape them onto the files, yang side up.

Pressing Down the Nasty 'Five Yellows'

Each year it is vital to note where the nasty 'five yellows' have flown. This part of time-dimension feng shui must be taken care of if you are to have career and prosperity success. The five yellows cause misfortunes to occur in the form of losses, setbacks, bad health and accidents.

The table below spells out the location of the five yellows over the next twelve years. This means that every year the afflicted direction/location changes, and you would be well advised to take note of this at the start of each lunar new year.

In 1999, the afflicted direction is the South. Thus the bad luck of this part of the house and office must be nullified if you are to have good luck. The best way to do this is to use a metal windchime to press down on the bad luck of the five yellows.

Positioning Windchimes

Windchimes used for this purpose should preferably have five solid rods. This creates a more melodious sound. Also, because the use of the windchime is not to channel chi upwards, it is not necessary to have windchimes with hollow rods. So in 1999 you should hang just such a windchime in the Southern part of your office and house.

It would be ideal, of course, if the toilet or kitchen were in the place or corner of the home that houses the five yellows. For instance, if the toilet is in the South, the house will enjoy better luck in 1999 since the toilet would have effectively pressed down on the bad luck of the South. However, it would also help to hang the windchime.

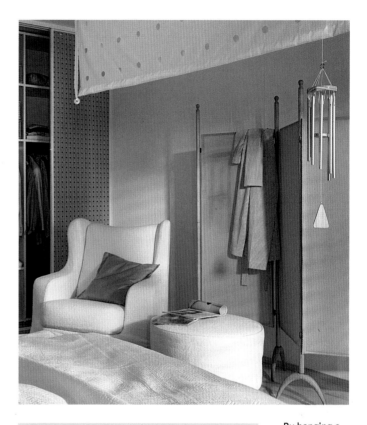

Where Are the Five Yellows

Year	Location of the Five Yellows
1999	South
2000	North
2001	South-west
2002	West
2003	South-east
2004	Centre
2005	North-west
2006	West
2007	North-east
2008	South
2009	South-west

By hanging a metal windchime (preferably five rod) in the five yellows' corner of your home (see chart), you can reduce your bad luck. The direction of the five yellows changes yearly.

97

The Prosperity Signature

A signature is said to attract great prosperity and success for a person if it starts with a firm upward stroke and then ends with another firm upward stroke. Check the signatures of any successful people that you know and, when you are convinced that this is correct, practise your own new signature until you achieve these auspicious strokes. The most auspicious signatures illustrated below are signatures A and C.

Signature A

From a feng shui perspective this will be the most auspicious signature of the four shown here. Note the upward starting stroke, and the upward ending stroke. This denotes a good beginning and a good ending to every project and job undertaken. My feng shui master tells me if you sign this type of signature forty-nine times on a wish list for forty-nine days, your wishes will come true!

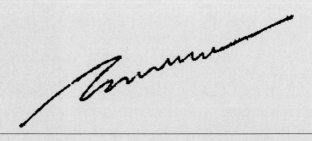

Signature B

This signature is only partly correct. It starts with a firm upward stroke but it ends with an equally firm downward stroke. Signatures that seem to end with a backward movement are not auspicious. It indicates a sad ending.

Signature C

This is another example of a signature that has excellent feng shui. Once again note that the beginning stroke is upward and the ending stroke is also upward. An ending upward stroke, which is a line under the signature, is also regarded as part of the signature. Thus those of you who do not have an upward ending stroke could include a firm line upward to create prosperity luck.

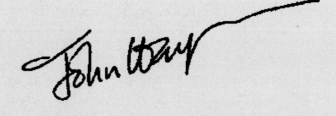

Signature D

This signature has an almost unnoticeable downward slant to its ending. It is therefore not auspicious. If your signature looks like this, try to change it so the stroke is moving upwards.

The Feng Shui of Watches and Clocks

The Chinese are very 'pantang', or deadly averse to, receiving watches and clocks as gifts. In fact, the older the recipient the more aggrieved he or she becomes when a clock is given as a birthday gift. This is because the timepiece is regarded as symbolic of the negative effects of time.

The clock, more than any other object, represents the passing of time. It is the antithesis of longevity symbols. As such, clocks are regarded as being extremely inauspicious objects around the office.

I remember years ago in Hong Kong when I nearly bought myself an antique grandfather clock for the office which I thought exhibited 'so much character', my feng shui expert friend strongly advised against the purchase. 'Very bad for business,' he said.

Watches and Clocks as Gifts

He told me that feng shui masters have attributed the fall of the Qing dynasty in China to the great many clocks the Qing rulers received as gifts from Western emissaries. These foreign visitors paid their respects at the Chinese Court and almost always brought along an elaborate European clock as a gift. No wonder all the young princes died! Indeed I myself have seen entire rooms full of these bejewelled clocks on display inside special rooms in the Forbidden City.

If you receive a watch as a gift, especially if it is a birthday gift, you should thank whoever gave it to you but immediately offer a token coin to nullify any negative effects. This symbolizes that you have immediately 'purchased' the watch from whoever gave it to you. According to advice given to me, it is perfectly acceptable for parents to give watches to their children as gifts but not the other way around.

Children should never give watches to their parents, grandparents or any of the older members of the family. Symbolically they are the opposite of the long-life symbols, like peaches and bamboo, the crane and the deer. A traditional, and welcome, Chinese gift to an elder of the family might be a painting of bamboo or a statue of the God of longevity.

> Watches are seen as negative presents by the Chinese, so, if you receive one as a gift, thank the person but give them a token coin back to prevent any bad effects.

PERSONAL GROOMING

99

Dress According to Your Five Elements

Work out the element shapes that are most auspicious for your KUA number (see bottom) and buy printed clothes that will help to increase your luck. If your good shape is round use different variations as below, but try to follow the productive cycle (see Tip 10).

Personalized feng shui has to do with the personal elements that rule our birth chart and these are usually viewed as a 'basket of elements' in accordance with our 'four pillars'. Each 'pillar' has 'two characters' and Chinese fortune telling is always referred to in terms of one's eight characters or *paht chee* chart. I have found that using the KUA numbers (see Tip 1) to identify the elements that work best for me is equally as effective as using the *paht chee* method which is very complicated to work out. Refer to Tips 1 and 11 to work out your KUA number and element. Then look at the list below and note the shape that will enhance your luck. Incorporate the rectangular, square, round, wavy or triangular shapes into the cut of your clothes as well as the patterns and prints you select for your ties, your shirts and so forth.

- Stripes are for those whose shapes are rectangular as denoted by the wood element.
- Triangles and A-line dresses are of the fire element.
- Square shapes denote the earth element.
- Round shapes and circles are of the metal element.
- Wavy shapes represent the water element.

Personalized feng shui can also be guided by the elements that are symbolized by our body shape, which changes as we age. First, you need to work out the shape that best describes you and then dress according to the productive cycle of the elements (see Tip 10). If your body shape is triangular i.e. small on top and heavy at the bottom then dressing with the rectangular shape in mind is excellent since wood (rectangle) produces fire (triangular).

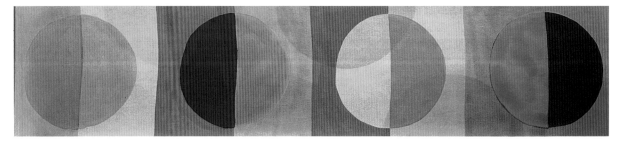

Five Element Shapes

Your Kua Number	1	2	3	4	5	6	7	8	9
Your success shape	I	■	▲	W	■	●	●	■	I
Your good health shape	I	●	W	▲	●	■	■	●	I
Your romance shape	▲	●	I	I	●	■	■	●	W
Your attractive shape	W	■	I	I	■	●	●	■	▲

Key
I stripes ■ square ● circle ▲ A-line W wavy

Balancing Elements With Shapes

Good feng shui in personal grooming can be achieved by skilfully balancing the elements that make up your total look. Combining shapes and colours in a way that ensure the elements stay in harmony can do this. The examples summarized on this page examines many combinations, both auspicious and otherwise. Check back to Tip 10 for the cycles of the elements.

- Long wavy hair always suggests the water motif. If your body shape is long and tall, then the element combinations suggest water and wood – a most auspicious combination as the elements are in harmony.
- Long wavy hair (water element) matched with a suit in blue, purple or black would mean too much water. The effect would then be unbalanced, and the feng shui not very good!
- If your body frame tends to be short and stocky, then wearing a straight tailored suit suggests an excess of the earth element since the overall shape is square. It would help if the suit is white (metal) since the combination or earth and metal would then be very auspicious.

Good feng shui in dressing always means good element harmony. The way to ensure you get this right is to look in the mirror and to pick out at least three items that represent element harmony. From the shape and texture of your hairstyle to the cut of your clothes, the colours and the patterns of your outfit you will be able to form an impression that seems harmonious or not.

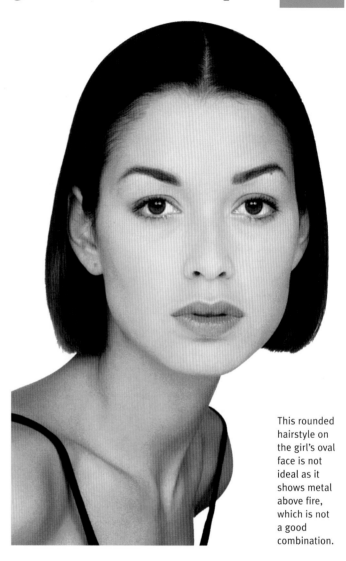

This rounded hairstyle on the girl's oval face is not ideal as it shows metal above fire, which is not a good combination.

Face and Hair Shape

- A rounded hairstyle on a rectangular-shaped face indicates metal on wood, so this is not a good style to have.
- A rounded hairstyle on an oval or heart-shaped face indicates metal above fire, which is a bad style to have.
- A rounded hairstyle on a square face represents metal above earth. This is a much better hairstyle as earth produces metal.

101 Avoid Combining Elements Destructively

It is always a good idea to memorize the element, or elements, that can harm you or which are discordant with your KUA number, or with your body shape (see Tips 1 and 11). Sometimes, when you check these various methods and formulae, it is possible that under one method, the element wood (rectangular, green) may be good for you and under another method it may be bad for you. When faced with such apparently contradictory indications, develop sensitivity to your own experience. Over time you will be able to isolate your good and bad colours, hairstyles and cuts of clothing.

Personal Feng Shui

For instance, I am a wood person because I was born in the year of wood. So green has always done wonders for me. Theoretically fire would not be good for me since fire burns wood. But I was a winter wood because I was born in the month of January, sorely in need of heat and warmth. I discovered that if I wanted high energy levels all I needed to do was dress in red. It never failed me. Red made me bloom and blossom. Apart from being a yang colour it complemented my personal feng shui needs perfectly.

Element Analysis

You should thus attempt to undertake your own personal element analysis in this way. Check against your KUA number to determine the colours that are harmful for you (see Tip 11) and then experiment. Thus if yellow (bright yellow is fire and light yellow is earth element) is bad for you, try wearing it and see

how the day goes for you. Do the same with prints and patterns, shapes and hairstyles.

Often, even if a colour shape or pattern in itself, may not be auspicious for you, the way you combine the elements in your total look can transform something bad into something good. When in doubt, undertake the element analysis I suggest earlier and let the elements in your grooming harmonize with each other.

Above When choosing your business clothes, think about how the elements' colours and symbolism work together to achieve the best combinations.

Pattern and Colour Combinations

Stripes:

- are extremely lucky when done in all shades of reds and maroon;
- are very unlucky when done in metallic colours or in white
- are very lucky when the background colour is blue or black
- of white on blue are lucky
- of white on gold or silver are bad
- of green on darker green is excessive wood and not good
- of green on black or blue are excellent
- of green on red denote success.

Wavy Lines:

- balance well with blues and greens
- are excellent against a white background
- clash with bright reds and orange
- mix well with dots and circles
- go well with rectangular shapes.

Dots:

- are best done in metallic colours, gold, silvers and white
- are auspicious on a beige or earthy background.

Zigzag Lines

- match well with orange, beige and browns
- are most auspicious on a background of green or brown.

Element Symbolism

In personal feng shui your build and everything you wear has element symbolism and connotations. The man in the picture's suit, shirt and tie all relate to the elements. Always work out if you are wearing too much of one element or if the combination of the elements is destructive.

Squares and Checks:

- match extremely well with reds and yellows
- match well with whites and metallic colours.
- are very inauspicious on a blue or black background.
- are not recommended in greens or blues.

PERSONAL GROOMING

103

Dirty, Torn Clothes Create Negative Vibes

One of the worst things anyone can do to undermine his or her feng shui is to wear dirty, torn clothes. Dressing with ripped out holes in your jeans, or going for the washed-out faded look may well make you look cool with the younger generation, but old fashioned Chinese like me will frown strenuously on this kind of dressing. Why? Simply because it brings such enormous bad luck. Dress like a down-and-out – and you will soon turn into one!

Dressing like this attracts poverty and bad luck vibrations that often translate into the most severe kind of ill fortune. My nephew and niece used to wear jeans with enormous cut outs and holes… and they had severe bad luck indeed! I advised them to get rid of them and to change their whole attitude towards dressing. They have since thrown out all their ripped clothing and their luck has changed.

Even when you have no plans to go out and even if you work from home, you should make sure that you never wear clothes that suggest that you are a slouch. When you wake up to face the day, get out of your pyjamas!

Take the trouble to change your clothes, wear your make-up and stay well groomed ready to greet in any good fortune that may come your way that very day!

Enhance Yang Energy
Wearing unflattering clothes creates unflattering energies. Such clothes deplete you of yang energy and cause you to feel lethargic and lacking in energy. Change out of your night clothes as soon as you wake up, and do throw out those shapeless unflattering so-called home clothes!

104

Never Hang Washing Out Overnight

Never hang washing to dry outside overnight as the clothes are said to absorb too much yin energy.

For as long as I can remember, the taboo of leaving clothes out overnight has been in my consciousness. From a young age I had been told that hanging one's clothes out at night attracted the energies of wandering spirits to get attached to the clothes so that when worn, the bad energies of these spirits would cause bad luck.

Those were, of course, old wives' tales. But, feng shui masters also warn against hanging clothes and other washing on the clothesline after dark. But their reasoning has greater appeal for me. They explain this taboo in terms of the clothes absorbing the excessive yin energies of the night. The same also applies to sheets and blankets.

It is for this same reason that feng shui practitioners of the East are often reluctant to hang clothes to dry in dark windowless rooms. They prefer to hang clothes out in the open air and during daylight. This allows clothes to absorb the positive yang energies of bright sunlight, rather than lifeless yin energy.

Good Grooming Makes Good Feng Shui

Being well groomed does not necessarily mean dressing to the heights of fashion. It does not mean dressing in designer clothes. Good grooming does not have to be expensive. It means presenting a balanced harmonious look to the world. It means having clothes that have fluid lines that look neat and are clean. All the guidelines for arranging one's space harmoniously apply with equal emphasis to one's appearance. And, as with space feng shui, good grooming feng shui also calls for balance and harmony.

Here are two important tips that apply to the feng shui of appearance.

Gold jewellery that is set with precious stones makes a very good feng shui combination as the stones are earth and the gold is metal, so one element generates the other. But do not wear too much jewellery as you will create an imbalance.

- Whether you wear the real thing or fabulous fakes, please remember that jewellery represents an excellent and most harmonious feng shui combination. This is because the mixture of the earth (stones) and the metal elements (gold, platinum and silver) also reflects the productive cycle of the elements.

- Wearing jewellery, and especially gold jewellery that is set with precious stones (diamonds, rubies, sapphires and emeralds) does represent excellent feng shui. So I usually encourage people to use accessories as adornments to one's appearance. But you should not overdo things. If you end up looking like a Christmas tree, the effect could be an excess of metal. The resulting imbalance of the elements then becomes harmful and is especially injurious to those born during the spring months and in years that are of the wood element. Too much gold kills woodborn people!

It is also better to look slightly prosperous and have some flesh on you than to look thin and scrawny. To the Chinese, being too thin is the surest indicator of bad luck. By the same token being just a tiny bit overweight (not flabby but full) is usually regarded as looking and being prosperous. Rich Chinese women who are first wives (called *tai tais*) are usually a little plump, as opposed to courtesans and concubines who are usually thin. Likewise, rich Chinese men almost always have a noticeable tummy. These are highly valued indicators of prosperity.

Wearing and Carrying Auspicious Accessories

Feng shui grooming takes account of the accessories you carry and wear since these add to your total look. See Tip 11 to check elements and colours.

Handbags

Ladies who carry handbags (or pocket books as they are called in the United States) can select them using feng shui knowledge to enhance their feng shui significance. Use the two standard benchmarks – shape and colour – to check the element combination of the bag. This should indicate if the bag has good or bad energy and therefore whether it has good feng shui. Rectangular bags in browns, blacks and greens are good. Square bags in beige, maroons, reds and yellows are also good. Circular ones in white, and beige are good.

Buttons

Buttons are usually round and when these are made of a metal, they represent strong metal element. Such buttons would be excellent for those wearing greens and browns. Plastic round buttons are basically harmonious.

Hats and Caps

Covers for the head signify shelter and are generally regarded as good feng shui. But hats and caps should not be black or blue in colour. This represents the water element for the head, which in feng shui is supposedly most inauspicious. Water above the mountain is one of the four danger indications of the *I Ching*. The great masters of feng shui interpret this to signify the danger of having the water

element on the head (of a person), and on the roof (of a property).

Ties and Scarves

These accessories have no feng shui significance except in the colours and patterns that are printed on them. Use the colour guides to apply element analysis to the wearing of ties and scarves.

Always choose accessories with feng shui principles in mind. For example, this woman has an auspicious black, rectangular handbag. However, her hat should be another colour as black on your head is not considered to be lucky.

Create Facial Balance With Make-up

Chinese matriarchs are great believers in the science of face reading, and would usually be reluctant for their sons to marry women whose faces indicated bad luck for their husbands. Bad luck faces are described as follows.

● Faces that do not have enough flesh; thus sunken cheekbones and the gaunt look popularized by the super-thin super models is usually dismissed as bad.

● Faces with too wide a jaw, to the extent that it looked angular. Square-jawed women are believed to 'eat their husbands', in other words, that their husbands will die at a young age, or at any rate long before them. In the old days, such women would usually have had a hard time finding husbands from good families.

● Faces whose eyes are too close together.

Such faces are deemed to be poverty faces. Those with this kind of face are believed to have hardships as they grow older. In other words their early life is better than old age.

● If a face has thick eyebrows, it would be considered even more negatively. Thin and well-shaped eyebrows are usually preferred and regarded more favourably than bushy eyebrows. Eyebrows should thus be trimmed and plucked to look less bushy.

The Chinese always viewed thick eyebrows with suspicion, so it is better to trim them regularly so that they are thin and well-shaped.

Using Make-up For Balance

In feng shui, what you perceive, i.e. what you actually see, is what is important. Thus it is possible to use make-up to correct features that are deemed to be bad feng shui.

● Firstly make sure faces are well balanced. Do not go for the high cheekbones so enamoured by the Western concept of beauty. Holes in the cheeks are deemed to be bad feng shui. Cheeks must look full, luscious and prosperous.
● Lips must be small but full.
● Noses should be high, round and fleshy. The more fleshy the nose, the more prosperity you will have!
● Jaws should be full. Small inadequate jaws indicate a short life.

The Feng Shui of Your Dressing Table

Your dressing table is best positioned in the South, South-west or North-east of your bedroom. Keep it well-lit for good energy, and make sure that the mirror does not reflect the bed which is not good feng shui.

The best feng shui feature at a dressing table is the presence of a bright light. This brings yang energy and also suggests the fire element. This brings a great deal of auspicious energy to your daily grooming ritual. If your dressing table is located in the South, South-west or North-east of your bedroom, this lighting feature will be even more auspicious.

Always make sure that your dressing table does not have its mirror directly facing your bed. This creates bad feng shui for you when you are sleeping. Try to make sure the mirror is placed in a way that does not reflect the bed. If it does, the mirror will bring you grief.

A mirror facing the bed is often the cause of a happy marriage going sour. You could suffer from problems caused by the entrance of one or more outside parties coming into the relationship. If you presently have a mirror facing your bed, cover the mirror at night with a tablecloth or completely reposition your dressing table.

Always sit facing one of your four good directions when applying your face make-up in the morning or before you go out at night. This means that as you stare at yourself in the mirror, you are staring into a direction that represents one of your auspicious directions according to the KUA formula in Tips 1 and 2. Not only will this bring you luck as you put on your face in the mornings, it will also put you in a most pleasant frame of mind.

The Feng Shui of Facial Enhancement

Having bright red cheeks on a fair-coloured countenance is almost always considered a face of good fortune. In the old days when make-up was less freely available, various herbal concoctions brought colour to the cheeks, lips and eyes of the young women of marriageable age.

Good Luck Faces

Rosy cheeks symbolized the promise of fertility which, in women was regarded as great good fortune. Rosy cheeks that were full and rounded were viewed as being even better fortune. Such cheeks indicate a life that gets better and more prosperous. So the modern day use of cheek colour is an excellent feng shui practice which I thoroughly encourage.

A fair complexion that had no blemishes was also considered a face of good fortune. Moles, freckles and other unsightly birthmarks were usually frowned upon as indicating obstacles in one's life. Moles at the back of the neck were especially frowned upon since this indicated a hard, burdened life.

Marks (including moles) on any part of the face, but especially along the centre line were considered indicators of hardships at various times of the person's life. Young women often got rid of these blemishes to enhance both their appearance as well as their good fortune. Modern make-up today can do the job less painfully!

Good fortune lips are supposed to be tiny and very red. Women who had naturally bright lips that were also small and dainty were highly regarded as great beauties and women of great good fortune. Large thick lips were considered a sign of poverty and represented a certain hardship in life. I hasten to add that I personally adore full lush lips despite this feng shui belief.

Good luck faces are usually round and rather plump. The jaw line should not be too wide since this indicates early widowhood.

Hair should be combed well back and adorned with gold ornaments. Hair that is parted in the centre indicates a life devoid of family. A well-adorned head attracts good fortune to a woman's family.

Face Reading

The Chinese believed that a woman's face showed signs of their good or bad fortune. Lips that would bring good fortune were supposed to be small and red. So, even if your lips are slightly fuller, wearing a red lipstick (as right) would be considered favourably.

The Dragon Symbol is All-powerful

The East is the place traditionally associated with the dragon and so placing a dragon image in the East always represents excellent feng shui. There are many ways to do this. You can use just one of the methods or, if you are like me, you can use a combination of several methods.

- Buy a dragon image and display it on a table or cabinet on the East side of your office or your study. It can be made of ceramic, crystal, or wood. Dragons made of gold, cloisonné or other metals are not encouraged since the metal element destroys the wood element. Also, never place the dragon inside the bedroom. It is too yang a creature to symbolize inside the bedroom which should be maintained as a restful place.
- Hang a picture of a dragon along the East wall of your office.

Placing a ceramic plate with dragon images (right) on a cabinet in the East side of your office is very fortuitous. If you are a dragon person, sitting on a chair with carved dragon images can be very energizing. The dragon is central to feng shui and where it is good the people are said to enjoy the dragon's precious cosmic breath.

- Simulate the green dragon of the East in your garden by having flowering plants set in a winding flowerbed on the East side of your garden.
- Use a table with dragons carved on the legs or a table with dragons inlaid in mother of pearl. This table can be your desk if you like but remember that not everyone has sufficient yang energy to sit at a dragon table. The same is true of a dragon chair. If you are born in the year of the dragon, the chances are that sitting on furniture carved with dragon images will greatly enhance your energy levels. But be careful. As I said previously not everyone has the personal luck to carry this off so if after sitting on a dragon chair you fall ill, then take it that it is not for you.
- Display ceramic bowls and art objects with the dragon image. These decorative objects are deemed to be extremely fortunate. You will find just such an object in every successful tycoon's office in the Far East.

The Phoenix For Successful Opportunities

The celestial phoenix is said to symbolize the luck of wish-fulfilling opportunities, and using it as a feng shui symbol is both easy and practical. It is especially effective when activating the luck of the South corner. Look for symbols, pictures and paintings of the phoenix, and try to get a picture of the phoenix without the dragon. To energize career luck, we do not want the dragon phoenix symbol since that symbolizes conjugal and marital happiness – a different type of luck.

Representing the Phoenix Symbol

On its own the phoenix symbolizes the coming of opportunities that bring success and prosperity. In feng shui the phoenix is represented by a small mound or slightly elevated land in the South, or in the front part of the home or office.

If you do not have a small mound in front of your front or main door it is a good idea to create one artificially to represent the phoenix. For activating the 'corners' of the office the symbolism of the phoenix can be contrived by using images of other well-plumaged birds like the cockerel, the rooster, the peacock or other majestic-looking birds.

This beautiful silk robe is decorated with glorious well-plumaged birds that resemble the phoenix. This can bring the wearer success in forthcoming opportunities.

The Celestial Phoenix

The phoenix is the king of all plumed creatures, and in Chinese mythology is often represented as the mate of the celestial dragon. When placed together, the phoenix and the dragon represent a happy marriage. So wedding banquets are often decorated with dragon phoenix images. We want the phoenix energy, which is yang on its own, but which becomes yin when it is placed beside the dragon.

112 Use Your Success Direction For Mentor Luck

Energizing your own sheng chi (or success) direction complements what you do in the North-west corner to attract mentor luck (see Tip 115). The latter method applies universally for everyone while the sheng chi direction is a personalized direction based on each individual's date of birth, and is therefore different for each individual.

If you want to ensure that your working life is filled with mentors and powerful patrons, it helps to activate your sheng chi and the best way to do this is to enter your office each day from your sheng chi direction. This means that each morning as you enter, good luck follows you into the office.

So if your sheng chi is East, you should try to make sure the door into your office is facing East. Obviously this is not always possible, in which case you will need to identify

If your sheng chi direction is in the North you can encourage mentors into your business life by placing a bowl or vase of water in that corner in your office.

your sheng chi location inside your office room, and then activate that corner according to the theory of the five elements. Check what your KUA number is by returning back to Tip 1 and then take the appropriate action according to the table here.

Energizing Your Sheng Chi

Your KUA number	Your sheng chi is	What to do
1	South-east	Place a lush plant or a water feature in your South-east corner.
2	North-east	Use a globe, a world map or natural quartz crystal to energize the North-east.
3	South	Install a very bright light in the South or decorate with something red.
4	North	Place a water feature – a bowl with water and a tortoise or a small fountain in the North.
5 male	North-east	Same as KUA number 2 shown above.
5 female	South-west	Same as KUA number 8.
6	West	Place a large metallic object in the West.
7	North-west	Hang a windchime.
8	South-west	Place a big decorative object made of ceramic in the South-west.
9	East	Same as KUA 1 above.

Activate All the Symbols of Protection

Getting ahead in one's career by catching the eye of a potential patron or mentor has a downside in that it can also make you an unwitting victim of office politics and corporate power struggles. It is therefore always advisable to activate at least some of the symbols of protection, and strenuously observe the feng shui guidelines that guard against getting stabbed in the back (see also Tip 114).

Probably the best symbol of feng shui protection is the usually benevolent white tiger that is the alter ego of the green dragon. According to feng shui, the white tiger is always present where the dragon is deemed to be, but he is there to protect. So the tiger must always be controlled by the green dragon. This means that the East side (the dragon) must always be higher than the West side (tiger).

Fu Dogs as Sentinels

In Chinese tradition, the most common symbols of protection are the pair of Fu dogs commonly found outside temples and important buildings. In recent years, exquisitely made ceramic Fu dogs have been coming out of China, and you may wish to invest in a pair to place as sentinels outside your office. I place a pair outside my home, but on the wall just outside my main door I also place an eagle poised in the attack position as well as a wonderful painting of a lioness. All work equally well.

Keep a Tiger on Guard

To activate the tiger as a symbol of protection, get a ceramic tiger or any other fierce member of the wild-cat family and place it outside your office. Do not place the tiger inside your office – unless your astrological chart makes you strong enough to have a tiger in your office. It could turn its fangs on you. It is much safer to place the tiger outside where it stands guard.

The head of a panther or leopard standing guard just outside your office door is also very effective as a symbol of protection. Be careful not to put something like this inside and facing you!

Traditionally in China Fu dogs are protective symbols. By positioning a pair of these dogs outside your office you will get protection in your working life.

114

Don't Get Stabbed in the Back

Never sit with your back to the door in a meeting or in your normal office environment as you will always feel threatened.

A great deal of good feng shui is about being defensive and watching behind you. This is to make certain you do not get stabbed in the back or caught unawares in a difficult situation. Specific feng shui guidelines deal with this, mainly concerning the way you sit.

A major taboo in feng shui for the office is never to sit with the entrance door behind you. It does not matter if the door is directly behind or at a slant to your desk. You should never sit in a position that makes it impossible to see who is entering your office. You should not let yourself be taken unawares at any time. If this is the way you are sitting now, I strongly advise you to move your desk around to face the door – even if by doing so you could well be sitting facing one of your inauspicious directions. This is how serious sitting with the door behind is. You will definitely be 'stabbed in the back' if your desk is not moved.

It is also advisable never to sit with a window behind you, unless your window is facing another building that can act as a firm support for you. Equally bad is sitting with a bookcase behind you that has exposed open shelves. These shelves act as blades cutting into your back. Make doors for the bookcase, or move the desk around or do both.

115

Use Your North-west For Patron Luck

When it comes to looking after your success luck, the most important part of your home, your study, or your office is the North-west sector. Not only is the North-west the sector that most affects the luck of the head of the family or company, this corner also governs the quality of your mentor and patron luck.

When the North-west of any room enjoys good feng shui balance and harmony, the people who use the room will find themselves being assisted by helpful patrons. There will be many 'heaven men' who will be the source of wonderful opportunities.

When I was in my twenties, and had just discovered feng shui, just for fun I would apply every little tip I received about energizing the North-west corner of my home and office.

I hung not one, but an entire row, of windchimes along the North-west wall of my home. In my office I hung another row of windchimes and I aimed a small fan at the windchimes so that tinkling music filled my office all the time. Amazingly, my career path became filled with countless mentors.

You can also hang a picture of a large mountain to symbolize the earth in this area as earth produces metal.

The Chien Trigram Brings Powerful Help

The trigram Chien is the most powerful of the eight feng shui trigrams. It represents heaven, the leader, the mentor and the patriarch. When you surround yourself with the Chien trigram you will be get precious yang energies since it is also the ultimate yang trigram. It has three solid black lines, unbroken and strong, as shown in the symbol. There are many delightful ways of achieving a roomful of Chien energy that will help you to attract powerful and helpful people into your life.

Cornices

One of the prettiest and most effective methods of surrounding yourself with Chien energy is to have plaster cornices on the ceiling of your office. These cornices comprise three solid lines of plaster that not only look attractive but are also good feng shui. It is not necessary to have any other kind of pattern on the ceiling, just three lines will do the trick.

A variation of this is to place the three-line cornices midway up the wall as a dado rail, but I prefer to have them as cornices as I do not like cutting my walls in half with a decorative divider.

A third way to energize Chien is to have a desk with cornices carved into the design. Energizing the Chien symbol on your work table is very powerful indeed.

Above The trigram Chien is the most powerful as it represents heaven.

Left You can utilize the energy of the Chien trigram in your office by featuring a cornice on the ceiling.

Protect Your Income With Feng Shui Coins

Tie three coins with red thread and put them in each handbag and wallet or purse you own. This is one of the best tips I have ever received concerning all the small little ways I could use three Chinese coins to activate and symbolize a never-ending source of income for myself.

I found it so effective that I started placing coins in all my purses and wallets and handbags. In the interest of fashion, I change my handbag frequently to match my clothes so, to make certain I was never short of cash, I put these feng shui coins in all my bags. I might add that it is not necessary to use more than three coins. In fact three is a very good symbolic number that represents the union of heaven, earth and man – itself an auspicious combination. Never use four or five coins since these are not regarded as lucky numbers. You may if you wish use six, seven or eight coins as all of these are all considered lucky numbers.

Giving Coins as Gifts

I have recommended this tip to many people and one of my favourite little gifts is to give a red packet with three coins tied with red thread to symbolize the offering of wealth luck to my friends. This is a very auspicious habit to cultivate since the act of giving is in itself most auspicious, especially when giving something as symbolically lucky as three coins in a red packet. Do this when you attend any auspicious occasions. Add the coins to the presents and gifts that you give to celebrate the weddings and birthdays of your loved family members and good friends.

Remember that it is the red thread that activates the yang energies of the coins and that by themselves, these coins do not have feng shui significance. If you do not have any red thread, you may use a bright red ribbon. It has the same effect although the Chinese view it as even more lucky when the coins have been expertly tied into never ending auspicious knots.

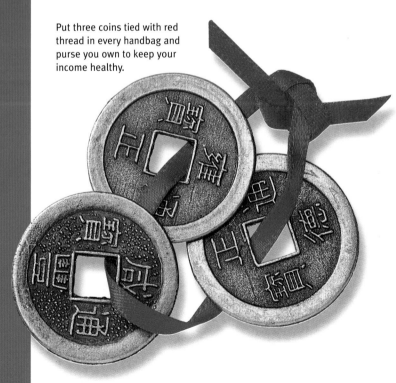

Put three coins tied with red thread in every handbag and purse you own to keep your income healthy.

At Work Sit Facing Your Success Direction

The most potent method of enhancing your wealth luck at work is to use Compass School feng shui, which reveals your sheng chi or most auspicious direction, based on your date of birth. To find out your personal sheng chi, first calculate your KUA number, using the formula in Tip 1. Then refer to the table in Tip 2 to identify your sheng chi direction. You must always try to sit facing this direction.

Auspicious Directions

Your Kua	Your Sheng Chi direction	Your other good directions
1	SE	N, S, E
2	NE	W, SW, NW
3	S	N, E, SE
4	N	S, E, SE
5	NE/SW	W, NW
6	W	NW, NE, SW
7	NW	W, NE, SW
8	SW	NW, W, NE
9	E	SE, N, S

Design an Auspicious Calling Card

Try to use feng shui dimensions in the design of your calling card. This means at least one side of the card should be less than 5.1 cm (2 in). Anything from this to 16.5 cm (6 1/2 in) is deemed inauspicious. My own calling card is less than 5.1 cm (2 in) in both width and length.

Be very careful when designing your corporate logo too. Never go for any design that is sharp, pointed or angular, especially if one of the points is inadvertently pointed directly at your company name. I strenuously warned a bank that had just such a logo. My advice was ignored and that bank was one of the casualties of the Asian economic crisis and now no longer exists. Also be careful about shapes. Rounded, curved shapes are always to be preferred over angular or triangular shapes.

If you have no choice in the matter of your company logo, then I strongly advise you to make certain that none of the angles are pointed directly at your name on the card. Move it right out of the 'firing range' if it is necessary.

Guidelines on Calling Card Colours

- Black printed on white is better than black printed on beige. So white calling cards are to be preferred to off-whites.
- When using two colours make certain the colours are harmonious. Good colour combinations are black with green, black with brown, black with blue, and black with metallic.
- Inauspicious combinations are black with red, black with orange, and black with yellow.

HARPER PR
245 Maddox Street
London SW1 3PD

SUSAN HARPER
MANAGING DIRECTOR
0171–879 3300/5

When designing your calling card, make sure that at least one of the sides is less than 5.1 cm (2 in) wide as these are auspicious feng shui dimensions.

120

Bury a Lucky Money Box in the West

This is the Chinese character for metal. It also represents silver and gold.

Feng shui speaks of the great value of burying a money box in the West or North-west. The symbolism that is created is most auspicious for the entire household, especially if there is also a small mound to represent a mountain. This symbolizes a mountain of gold in one's backyard. Since earth produces gold in the cycle of elements, this method of energizing feng shui is deemed to be doubly auspicious.

The money box can be represented by the strong box or safe of modern times. So, if you have a safe, it is a good idea to place it in the West or North-west – both of which corners represent the metal element. The Chinese character for metal, shown here is also the character for gold, which in turn represents wealth. The North-west is also the place of the father of the family family, so energizing the North-west is excellent feng shui for the entire family.

If you have a garden, you can bury a money box, preferably filled with coins, in the West part. You can use leftover change to fill up your money box, but higher denomination coins are better than pennies. Chinese coins with the yin yang characters and the square hole in the centre are best.

121

A Sailing Ship Loaded with Gold

The sailing ship has always been a symbol of success in business. In the old days many old-style Chinese entrepreneurs used the sailing ship as their logo since this symbolized the winds bringing more business, more trade and therefore more turnover. Indeed, next to the dragon, the sailing ship is the most popular symbol that is used by Chinese businessmen.

To energize your feng shui luck for the office, place a model of a sailing ship in the vicinity of the entrance door. You must then make very certain that the sailing ship is sailing inwards, towards the inside of the office. Do not let the sailing ship face outwards, as if it is sailing away. This is vital! Symbolically the ship must be coming in, not going away! The same thing can be done at home. Get a sailing ship and display it near your front door.

Please note that a ship with sails to 'catch the wind' is deemed more auspicious than a model of the Titanic, which, as everyone knows, sank into the Atlantic Ocean. The symbolism of the sails catching the wind and bringing gold to you is most auspicious. So, if you wish to use this tip, shop carefully for the right kind of sailing ship. The next thing to do is to fill the ship with gold. Imitation gold ingots, which you can buy for a song, are easily available in Chinese emporiums. Stack them up inside the ship. If you cannot find these fake gold ingots, then place coins and money inside the ship.

A Personal Wealth-enhancing Water Dragon

The feng shui dragon is a most auspicious creature, and creating a water dragon in the home is one of the best ways of energizing wealth luck. The ancient classical texts on water dragons are so important in feng shui it would take an entire book comprehensively to explain the many variations of successfully building a water dragon.

However, it is possible to create a personal water dragon, using plants and the presence of flowing water. A mini fountain is the most suitable habitat for a water dragon in the living room. Get a small gold dragon and place it in a fountain, allowing the water to flow over the dragon.

You should identify the exact spot in your living room where this water fountain will bring you the best of luck. Based on the calculations of fey sin or flying star, for this the period of 7, i.e. from now until the year 2003, water fountains are best placed in either the North, East, South-east, or South-west. These are the only four locations that are auspicious during this period of time. The best place for your water fountain depends on the exact direction your main door faces. Use the table here to determine your best location out of the four possibilities.

A boy scout compass will enable you to measure the degree. Note that each direction has three sub-directions.

Placing Your Water Dragon

Direction which the main door faces	Bearing exact degrees	Best location for water fountain
South1	157.5- 172.5	North
South 2/3	172.5- 187.5	North
North1	337.5- 352.5	North
North 2/3	352.5- 007.5	North
East 1	067.5- 082.5	East
East 2/3	082.5- 097.5	East
West1	247.5- 262.5	East
West2/3	262.5- 277.5	South-west
South-west 1	202.5- 217.5	North
South-west2/3	217.5- 232.5	South-east
South-east1	112.5- 142.5	South-east
South-east 2/3	127.5- 142.5	South-west
North-east1	022.5- 037.5	East
North-east 2/3	037.5-052.5	South-west
North-west1	292.5- 307.5	North
North-west2/3	307.5- 322.5	South-east

The dragon is one of the best creatures to bring fortune to people in feng shui. To bring in some dragon luck for yourself, you can create a water dragon in your living room sitting it in one of the auspicious corners.

123 Create a Personal Wealth Vase

This is a very personalized tip passed to me by a practising feng shui master from Taiwan. It was during my corporate career days in Hong Kong. He told me that he often advised his rich clients each to create a personal wealth vase to preserve their wealth.

Get a beautiful and valuable vase, he advised. A vase made of the earth or metal elements would be acceptable. Earth element vases would be porcelain or crystal while metal element vases would be made of either copper, brass, silver or gold. Needless to say, the more expensive the material, the more auspicious the vase. So a gold vase would be infinitely more auspicious than a silver one which, in turn, would be more auspicious than copper or brass. It was also acceptable to have silver gold-plated vases since a solid gold vase would be much too expensive to buy.

Fill your wealth vase with precious gems – or semi-precious stones like crystals, quartzes, amethysts, citrines, tiger's eye, lapis lazuli, malachite, pearls, and so forth. Put your jewellery inside your wealth vase too.

Locating Your Wealth Vase

I personally used a crystal vase, filled with semi-precious stones, to make my wealth vase. As this was of the earth element I placed it in the earth element corner of a cupboard in my bedroom, i.e. the South-west corner. The North-east is also acceptable. For those who opt for metallic vases, place them in the West or North-west corners.

Please note that the personal wealth vase should be kept hidden away, inside a cupboard in your bedroom. The wealth vase must never face the front door since this symbolizes wealth draining away. You should never show anyone your wealth vase.

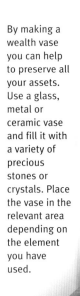

By making a wealth vase you can help to preserve all your assets. Use a glass, metal or ceramic vase and fill it with a variety of precious stones or crystals. Place the vase in the relevant area depending on the element you have used.

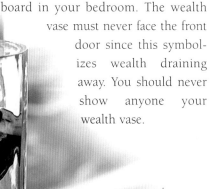

Invite the God of Wealth Into Your Home

The Chinese have several deities they regard as the wealth god. Probably the most popular is the god of wealth featured below and it is this god of wealth I have 'invited into my home. I have also recommended, it with huge success, to many friends of mine.

His name is Tsai Shen Yeh and he is often depicted sitting on a tiger to symbolize his control over this animal. In the lunar years of the tiger, displaying this wealth god is said to particularly auspicious.

I do not worship or pray to this deity. Instead I treat his presence in my home as purely symbolic. For good measure, I also hang a specially knotted cluster of nine Chinese coins, tied with red thread, to activate the prosperity attributes of the coins.

Locating the God of Wealth

The best place to locate the god of wealth is on a table or sideboard that is between 76–83 cm (30–33 in) high and directly facing the front door. So, the first thing you see upon coming into the home is the wealth god. He greets the chi (or energy) coming into the home, transforming it into healthy prosperous energy that flows through the house. If it is not possible to place the god here then put him in the corner of the living room that is diagonally opposite the entrance door. The god of wealth should still face the front door. Please do not place him in your bedroom or dining room. Another deity usually regarded as bringing wealth is the equally popular Kuan Kung. Another great favourite is the Fat Laughing Buddha shown on the right.

This Fat Laughing Buddha can also be included in your home. He can bring lots of success and help to take away any problems.

Placing Your God

A statue of the wealth god, Tsai Shen Yeh, can be placed in the corner of your living room that is diagonally opposite the door.

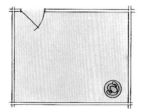

Place your god here

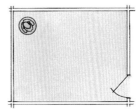

Place your god here

A Three-legged Frog For Luck

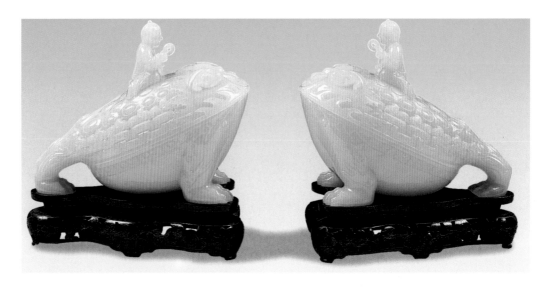

Right These jade frogs symbolize good fortune and can be put in the living or dining room, but always make sure they face inwards.

Below The three-legged frog with a coin in his mouth is best positioned diagonally opposite the front door under a table.

Frogs and toads are generally regarded as auspicious creatures to have around the garden, and the Chinese believe that, if there is a whole family living in your backyard, you will be protected from any dangers or bad luck which might be coming your way.

It is the three-legged frog, however, that is supposed to be extremely auspicious, and it is easy to find these good fortune symbols in any Chinese supermarket. The three-legged frog is usually depicted as having three coins in its mouth to signify him bringing gold into your home. This same symbolism can also mean taking gold out of the house. So the way the frog is placed becomes very important.

Position the three-legged frog symbol near the vicinity of the front door but facing inwards, as if it has just come into the house. Do not allow the frog to be placed directly facing the door. This symbolizes gold going out of the house. It is also best to place the frog at the far corner diagonally opposite the main door. Put it under a table inside a cupboard or hidden away under chairs and other furniture.

Avoiding Bad Luck Chi

Frog symbols should not be placed in the kitchen or any of the bathrooms and toilets. In these inauspicious places the frog turns malevolent and, instead of bringing good fortune, they tend to attract bad luck chi that cause havoc with the energy of the home.

It is also not a good idea to put them in the bedrooms. They are best when placed in either the living or dining areas of the home and, remember, never facing out, always facing in!

Keep a Pet Terrapin For Good Fortune

It is possible to attract good fortune and luck into the home by keeping pet terrapins. These beautiful domesticated mini-tortoises can be purchased from fish shops, and they make excellent pets for young children. When the children grow up, these terrapins usually lie forgotten in their little ponds. Nevertheless, because they are such hardy reptiles, they live on growing slowly and not requiring very much care.

Terrapins bring great good fortune and protection to households that keep them. In old China, many of the imperial palaces and homes of wealthy mandarins had terrapin ponds. In Malaysia, terrapin ponds can be seen in the Kek Lok Si temple in Penang Hill, and also in the Genting Highlands.

On an individual level, anyone can tap into the luck of the terrapin. Do not forget that this humble reptile is regarded as a very auspicious celestial creature believed to be imbued with strong protective powers. For this reason, I keep a pet terrapin and he lives in a large ceramic pot that is kept in the North part of my home.

Caring For Your Terrapin

Use a decorative ceramic or porcelain pot that is at least 20 cm (18 in) in diameter. Keep it half-filled with water and place a small rock in the centre. This allows your terrapin the choice of being in or out of the water.

Remember that terrapins are reptiles. Change the water three times a week and always let tap water stand for a while for the chlorine to evaporate. Feed with fish food or fresh green vegetables.

It is not necessary to keep more than one. Since one is the number of the North location, and the terrapin in feng shui is associated with the North, a single terrapin represents excellent feng shui. Do not worry that the terrapin will feel lonely. This is a creature who is a natural loner and is happiest when alone. If the terrapin you keep dies, simply get another one. This simply means your pet has successfully protected you from a minor disaster.

You can bring more good luck into your life by keeping a terrapin. They happily live in large ceramic pots with some water and a rock inside. Put your terrapin in the North corner of your home for the best protection.

127 Make a Better Turnover With Tinkling Bells

In the olden days, bells usually symbolized the announcement of good news and hence were symbols of good fortune. Chinese shop-keepers have always known about the efficacy of tinkling bells to attract customers into their shops. These little metal bells create good chi (or energy) each time someone opens the door to come in, in the process bringing in the luck required to enhance the shop's turnover. This method is especially effective for shops selling personal items and products like jewellery, clothing and accessories.

The tinkling bells can be made of any kind of metal and to increase their effective-ness they should be tied with a red ribbon to activate their intrinsic yang energy. The ideal number of bells is six or seven although most shopkeepers usually keep only one pair.

There are two methods of hanging these bells to the doors:

● attached to the door handles on the outside of the shop
● attached high above the door in such a way that each time the door opens the bells will then sound.

Tiny tinkling bells can also be placed inside the shop, anywhere along the West or North-west walls or directly facing the entrance door, placed high on the ceiling. This serves to entice the good chi to enter into the shop. These bells do not have to be seen. Their presence in the shop is symbolic and, after you have placed them there, you can just forget about them.

128 Stick Three Lucky Coins on Your Cash Box

Old Chinese antique coins, particularly those from the Chien Lung period of the Ching Dynasty, have many different uses in the practice of feng shui. If you cannot get hold of the antique variety, imitation Chinese coins can also be used for all your feng shui enhancements related to increasing your wealth and income luck. Whatever coins you use, always make sure that you wash them with sea salt before you start to use them. This gets rid of any negative energy that may still be clinging to them. This is merely a precau-tion and you should not fret if you have

already started using these coins and did not do this. Imitation Chinese coins from feng shui kits do not have any negative energies attached to them.

The best way to use the coins is to tie three coins in a straight line, with the yang side (the one with four sides) facing upwards, and then tape them with transparent cello-phane tape on to your cash box to increase your daily take from cash sales. You can also stick three coins inside your cash register or on the cover of your invoice book. This is a very effective way of generating better sales.

Reflect the Till in a Wall Mirror

Chinese shopkeepers are fervent believers in placing large wall mirrors inside their shops. This not only doubles the products on display, thereby signifying the prosperity of a well-stocked shop, but also creates massive doses of yang energy because it doubles all activity within the shop. Mirrors do wonderful things for business income when they reflect the cash register. It literally symbolizes a doubling of turnover.

Magnify Good Business Energy

Do not use a tiny little hand-held mirror, like a friend of mine did when I passed on this tip to her. I recall her telling me she did not believe in feng shui because she said my tip did not work. And then, quite by chance, I went to her shop and saw her pathetic little mirror! It was no wonder the mirror did not work. What it was reflecting was not the cash register but the door! So all the good fortune chi entering her dress shop was going right out again! I made her install a wall mirror in the correct way and since then she has had no complaints.

The use of mirrors is an excellent way of magnifying all the good energy of your business. If you have pillars, wrap them with mirrors, and if you have display cabinets, also wrap them with mirrors. And, if possible, place mirrors on all the walls around the shop except those directly opposite the entrance. This way all the products displayed will be reflected in the mirrors as well as all customers. This doubles the good fortune.

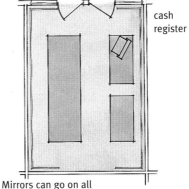

cash register

Mirrors can go on all walls, except the one which reflects the door

Mirrors are very useful in businesses when they are fitted on all walls to reflect the cash register (left and below) as they create the effect of doubling the profits. However, the wall opposite the door should be free of mirrors as the door should not be reflected in them.

Three Tips for Good Shop Layout Design

When you are designing the layout of your shop be mindful of these three important feng shui tips. You can be as creative as you wish, and you can use any kind of colour scheme that pleases you but observing these three tips will bring your shop excellent feng shui.

- You should let your shop door open into a small empty space or 'bright hall' where there are no cabinets, screens or furniture to block the chi entering the premises.
- You should select shapes for your display cabinets according to the corners where they are placed, making sure that you do not position any cabinet or table with the sharp edge pointed at the entrance door. (See Tip 10 for more on elements and compass direction.)
- If you want customers actually to buy your products once you have succeeded in enticing them in, you must design a traffic flow within the shop that meanders rather than moves in straight lines. Meandering traffic is simply excellent for business.

Placing Shop Units

When planning a shop design always place units in such a way that people can meander around them as shown here, in the same way that chi should. Work out the elements of the corners where units are going and then have them designed to that shape. Allow a small empty space just inside the shop entrance so that the chi has an uncluttered entrance.

Display the Lucky Horseshoe Shape 131

I find it really interesting that the horseshoe is regarded as a good luck symbol in the West. In feng shui the shape of the horseshoe very eloquently describes the ideal land configuration. It is a perfect representation of the green dragon/white tiger configuration that defines feng shui. Thus hanging a horseshoe is also considered favourably by feng shui.

The horseshoe shape, however, is regarded as particularly auspicious when used for display cabinets in retail shops, or when incorporated into wall designs. Simply hanging a specially designed wall cabinet that has been fashioned into the horseshoe shape is considered very lucky indeed. However, it is also important that you place the shape correctly. Do not let it directly face the entrance door, and definitely do not place the rectangular part of the shape directly facing the door.

Other Lucky Shapes

Other regular shapes like the rectangle and the square are also auspicious for display cabinets. Just make sure the sharp edges are never pointed to the door or the cash register.

The Pa Kua shape (octagonal) is also very lucky. It is excellent for displaying small items of high value like jewellery and accessories. The Pa Kua shape can also be elongated without losing its essence.

Circular shapes are also excellent and can be round or oval. These shapes do not have sharp edges and they are well balanced.

132

Hang Bamboo For Long-term Good Fortune

The bamboo plant is one of the most popular and potent symbols of longevity. It represents strength in circumstances of adversity and the ability to go through all kinds of stormy weather. Used as a feng shui tool it does not just symbolize long life and good health. The bamboo is also a very powerful sign of good fortune. It is always good feng shui to have a painting of the bamboo in the house or office. When you hang the bamboo stem in your shop it creates excellent protective and good fortune chi inside your shop. Your business will survive hard times and flourish in good times.

One way of bringing long-term good fortune into your shop is to hang the powerful feng shui symbol of a pair of bamboo stems above your shop entrance.

Re-creating the Pa Kua Shape

The hollow stem of the bamboo plant has many different feng shui applications and one of the easiest methods of activating the long-term good fortune of the bamboo is to hang a pair of bamboo stems above the entrance of the shop. The bamboo stems are placed tilted towards each other to simulate the Pa Kua shape. The bamboo stems are also tied with red ribbon to energize them.

It is not necessary to place too many of these bamboo stems in your shop. One pair is good enough and, if you find it difficult to place them above the entrance door, another good location is on the wall opposite directly facing the entrance door. These stems need not be too large nor too fat. A small 15-cm (6-in) piece will be good enough but make certain before you hang them that both ends are open.

Good Feng Shui Design For Restaurants

Traditional Chinese restaurants are the best places to go to if you want to see feng shui motifs being incorporated into restaurant design. The dominant colour used will always be red because the restaurant business is deemed to belong to the fire element. There will also be excellent lighting and round pillars will usually have colourful carved dragons and phoenixes on them. These Chinese restaurants of another time are getting scarce nowadays as the modern look takes over.

These days I have seen restaurants that use not the fire element in their décor but rather the water motif. As to be expected, those who have opted for the water rather than the fire motif for their restaurant business seem to be doing extremely well, especially in their dinner sittings. This is because

Many modern restaurants above and right are incorporating the colour blue into their decor. They may not always realize it, but by doing this they are bringing in the water motif which helps increase their sales of alcohol.

such restaurants have liquor licences and incorporating a water motif or pattern in the restaurant seems to give a huge boost to the wines and spirits side of things.

Fire Symbols For the Property Business

If you are in the property business feng shui should be of particular importance to you since you will have to advise customers on how the feng shui of any property can be improved. I am so often asked to give my opinion on pieces of property by my friends, and I try to tell them that most properties in the city have what I term very average feng shui – usually not very good, but also not bad. I have always advised that it is what you do with the property and how you decorate it which makes it good or bad for you.

The Feng Shui of Your Property

There are, of course, also the directions and orientations to take account of. Depending on your personal good luck directions some houses will obviously represent better luck for you than others. Having said that, there are buildings and houses where the feng shui is seriously afflicted by the proximity of lethal 'poison arrows'. The particularly difficult ones to counter are structures like transmission towers, a huge wall, a flyover, an elevated road, a water tank, a massive building or an oncoming road. These types of man-made structures are all found in the city and their negative energy is really very tough to overcome or diffuse. As an estate agent you should be wary about recommending or taking on properties affected by these structures.

Good feng shui for those in the property business requires the fire symbol. This is because in the productive cycle of relationships (see Tip 10) the fire element produces earth. And earth symbolizes property. Fire symbols usually mean that an estate agent's office should:

- be well lit – especially the foyer area and the area around the entrance door
- have something red. This can be one wall or a door painted red. Or it can be red curtains or a red carpet, or even a painting that is predominantly this colour
- incorporate the sun symbol.

Right For people working in the property business the best building to achieve success in is a triangular-shaped one. This is because this shape symbolizes the element fire which produces earth – property.

A Plant in the East Ensures Growth

In Feng Shui plants that have succulent leaves are always regarded as auspicious – such as the jade plant which is only one of a vast variety of succulents. Also, plants with rounded leaves are much better than those with long, straight or pointed leaves.

The lime plant is especially auspicious because the fruits are considered to symbolize gold. During the lunar new year many Chinese homes in Hong King, Singapore and Malaysia display at least two such plants, dripping with fruits, on both sides of the front door.

This is also an especially favourite method of energizing continued prosperity for businesses. So Chinese shopkeepers and business people in Hong Kong, Singapore and Malaysia also always display a pair of lime plants fruiting during the new year.

In the East shopkeepers place pairs of fruiting lime plants outside their shop during the New Year to help increase their prosperity. You can place a fruiting plant in the East of your shop to ensure that you have continuous growth of your business.

Wood for Growth

Plants belong to the wood element and the main connotation of wood is healthy and continuous growth. Placing all growing and healthy plants in the East and South-east energizes these two corners. Since the South-east is generally regarded as the wealth corner it is always good feng shui to have lush plants in this corner. It is however important to remember that dried plants or plants that look like they are dying or are unhealthy should be removed as sickly plants always give rise to excessive yin energy.

Balance the Elements of Your Business

If yours is a jewellery business try to make all your display cabinets curve. This is because the gemstones and jewellery business belong to the metal element and will thus benefit hugely from the curved shape. Let traffic move in a curved fashion inside your shop, and avoid red in your décor. This is because fire destroys metal and is not good for this business. Earth energies, on the other hand, will benefit you so do place objects made of clay and crystals.

The Antiques Business

If you are in the antique business, selling Buddhas and other decorative items collected from exotic places, you should be careful when handling deities and religious artefacts. Buddhas, for instance, and statues of ethnic gods should always be treated with respect. Remember that these are holy objects, which carry a great deal of symbolic energy. Place them on tables elevated at least higher than the people moving around the shop. The sleeping Buddha, for example, should never be placed on the ground. Nothing brings greater misfortune than disrespect shown to holy objects. So if you are in this business do be careful. Also, since you are dealing with antiques that give off a lot of yin energy, it does help if you create some yang energy in your shop. Keep the shop well lit. Let there be music in your shop, and

even paint one of the walls a yang colour such as white, red, yellow or orange.

A Souvenir Shop

If yours is a souvenir shop selling curios and other decorative objects made of wood, you might want to activate the wood energies of your shop. Bring in a nice bushy plant. It can be fake but it should look fresh and vigorous. This will tremendously enhance your turnover. Place a bright light just outside your entrance to create yang energy.

Right If you have a shop that displays images of religious deities, always make sure that they are placed high up and never on the ground as it is considered disrespectful.

Earth Energy Brings Good Fortune

If you want your business to benefit from earth energy, you should energize the three earth corners of your shop. These are:
- the Centre
- the South-west corner
- the North-east corner.

Place ceramics, pottery and crystals in these corners, either as decorative ornaments or as furniture.

Earth energy is strongest in the South-west. Place a small collection of pottery in this corner and shine a bright light to activate its energies. It is more effective if the light is red in colour since this strengthens the fire element that produces earth.

Mother of pearl furniture is an excellent energizer for the wood corners which are South-east or East. Chinese furniture also seldom uses nails, which are deemed to be bad luck when used in furniture. This belief can be traced to the five elements and their destructive cycle. Metal is said to destroy wood and, in the old days, emperors and rich mandarins alike would not sit on chairs or sleep on beds that had any nails driven into them.

Below Mother-of-pearl tables can really help to energize the earth corners of your shop, so display them in the Centre, the South-west corner or the North-east corner.

138 Guard Your Corporate Signboard

The corporate signboard is one of the most important things any successful business must protect against bad feng shui. Together with the main door, these represent the two things most vulnerable to negative energies that may be present in the surrounding environment. The first golden rule is to make sure that the signboard carrying your corporate name is placed high up on your corporate building. The corporate name should not be placed at ground level. It will cause the eventual demise of the company.

Even when your signboard is placed high on your building, the following are some structures you need to watch out for as they may harm it:

● elevated highways and flyovers
● transmission and other towers
● neighbouring buildings
● elevated city railways
● sharp edges of buildings.

If you have a large business it will benefit, and be protected from failure, if you place a well-lit signboard high above the ground. A signboard at ground level has negative energies.

Lucky Numbers Bring Prosperity

In New York, all the buildings have their numbers prominently displayed on the front of the building. It is perhaps a requirement of the city and it works really well for all those buildings with auspicious numbers, while working against those that are displaying what are considered 'death' numbers.

Auspicious Numbers

These are numbers that end with all the lucky numbers: 1, 6, 7, 8 and 9.

Each of these five numbers is a very lucky

number, but the number 8 seems to be the most popular simply because the word for it sounds like 'phat' which means prosperous growth in Chinese. The number 9 is regarded as the premier number by most feng shui masters because it signifies the fullness of heaven and earth. The number 9 never changes no matter how many times it is multiplied by itself. 9 times anything always leads to 9: 9 x 3 = 27 and 2 + 7 = 9 and so on. You can test this out yourself and see the power of 9.

The numbers 1, 6 and 8 together, in any order, are regarded as a most splendid combination representing enormous good luck, while the number 7 is lucky because it is the number that represents the period of time we are currently experiencing. It will cease being a lucky number by the year 2003, after which

8 becomes the number of the next period i.e. between 2004 to 2023. It is for this reason that the number 8 is regarded with such favour – because it represents both current and also future prosperity.

Unlucky Numbers

The number 4 is extremely unpopular because it is thought of as the death number simply because it sounds like 'die' in Chinese. For many people, however, the number 4 has brought tremendous good luck!

In feng shui numbers 2 and 3 together is considered a hugely bad combination leading to misunderstandings that can bring about severe problems in someone's life. But worse than that is the dreaded number 5. When the 5 appears in certain feng shui charts it is said to bring huge problems.

If your business has a lucky number, such as this one, always display it prominently so that you bring in good fortune.

Auspicious Corporate Logos

A corporate logo should always be designed with an eye to its feng shui significance. There are some general guidelines that are useful to follow and, if you have your own business, you might want to pass on these criteria to your art director or advertising agency.

Corporate symbols on buildings should always be planned carefully.

- Circular and curved designs are safer than designs with sharp edges and angles. Thus triangles and zigzags are not advisable. Please note that companies with an angular graphic as a logo that do actually do well always have their angles pointed outwards and never at their corporate name. The Hong Kong Bank's logo is an excellent example of a pointed logo that works in favour of the company.

- The use of animals in corporate logos usually signifies courage, strength and resilience. The dragon is the ultimate auspicious logo and most companies using the dragon usually go from strength to strength. The two companies I worked with had excellent dragon logos. I designed both logos, making the Hong Leong dragon fat and pregnant to symbolize the group's ambitions of becoming a global conglomerate giving birth to many subsidiaries. That was over fifteen years ago and the group is today a most successful global corporate player. I also designed the logo of Dragon Seed, my department store. Here I wanted a happy dragon, suggestive of quality. In both cases I made the dragon poised for flight upwards – suggesting soaring ambitions. Other animal logos would be the tiger and the lion but neither will ever be able to match the dragon in auspiciousness.

- The use of abstract designs and shapes – squares, circles and other five-, six- or eight-sided shapes – need careful thought. These can create extremely bad negative connotations resulting in bad feng shui.

- The use of flowers is excellent but can never be as powerful a symbol as a living creature. A bud about to open is more auspicious than a fully opened flower, in the same way that suggestions of spring colours (green) are always more auspicious than the colour of autumn (oranges and browns). One denotes a business about to take off while the other describes a business about to die. In the same way sunrises are always to be preferred to sunsets.

Grand Entrances For Excellent Feng Shui

The grander your corporate building, the grander should be the main entrance door – otherwise there will be no balance. Residents of large buildings that have small doors cannot have big luck. There is insufficient to go around. The good energy cannot enter the building in sufficient quantities.

A grand entrance is one that looks imposing and firm. It should preferably be properly decorated with guardian lions, high columns or other equally solid-looking or protective features. Having said this, do not overdo things. It is also important to understand that when the main door is too big, the building becomes overwhelmed with too much energy. This is often more dangerous than an insufficiently big door.

It is also a very good idea to install a pair of symbolic protective creatures. Many successful businesses in the Far East have guardian Fu dogs placed on guard outside the entrance of their buildings. The Hong Kong Bank has its famous pair of giant lions. These British lions were fashioned as replicas of the lions in Trafalgar Square in London but they have successfully protected the fortunes of the Hong Kong Bank since its founding in the nineteenth century.

A grand entrance to an office building always looks impressive to clients. It should be protected with columns, small bushes, a pair of lions as above, or any other solid feature.

Beware of Inauspicious Shapes

Building Shapes

Pyramid shapes, generally, are not a good idea for corporate buildings as they emit too much yin energy. But the Louvre pyramid, shown here, is ideal for a museum which does not need yang energy. It is also made from glass and lets in lots of positive energy from the sun.

Tycoons who have the resources to build large buildings – corporate headquarters, hotels and shopping malls – are usually too busy to bother about feng shui. Thus, large developments with serious feng shui mistakes do get built and usually with serious consequences for the companies that built them.

In Malaysia we have a shopping mall with an entrance fashioned to resemble a lion. It was meant to be the Sphinx but later became a lion. I am sure the owners should not be too surprised that no one likes shopping inside the belly of a lion!

The Auspicious Pyramid Shape

I have also seen the pyramid shape become increasingly popular. These shapes have tremendous impact on the surrounding environment. They emit energies that are not suitable for a living environment. The pyramid

(and the Sphinx) are reminiscent of tombs, and tombs are very, very yin places. Pyramid-roofed buildings that house corporate head offices can cause the eventual demise of these companies. One pyramid that is excellent feng shui, however, is the Louvre museum pyramid. It is lucky because of the way it was built. It is made of glass and it lets in masses of sunlight. Also, museums benefit hugely from yin energy.

The Sydney Opera House has shapes that suggest the fire element. It is therefore a very yang building and is a lucky building. However, being built by the sea puts fire with water. The good fortune is thus tempered by the element imbalance. The leaning tower of Pisa is round and this is suggestive of metal. Round buildings like this are not as auspicious as rectangular buildings which have more vibrancy.

Head Offices Must Have Solid Foundations

One very severe feng shui affliction has to do with the presence of empty space in some of the modern high-rise buildings that are being built today.

These 'holes' cause the chi to flow away rather than towards the building. If your corporate head office is built with the ground level exposed in this way, any good fortune that is destined to come your way, simply flows away again.

Such buildings are described as 'lacking in foundation'. The affliction becomes even more severe if the boardrooms and offices for the top brass of the company, i.e. the directors, are located in the part of the building that has nothing but empty space below.

Buildings like this also lack a proper entrance door, which signifies that the property has 'no mouth' where the good luck can enter. If your building has this feature, I suggest building walls and making use of your ground floor level. Otherwise the emptiness will cause the offices above to close down or go bust.

Modern Buildings

Although architecturally the modern design of Richard Rogers' Lloyds building in London has been greatly praised, in feng shui terms its design is not perfect. The solid pillars in this famous building have a very negative effect on the shops that directly face it. Also the internal escalators create much poisonous breath – shar chi. The empty space in the centre, which operates like an atrium, tends to allow chi to dissolve but because of the shar chi being created by the criss-crossing escalators it actually helps to alleviate the problem.

144 Check the Position of Your Building

Every corporate building should observe the general guidelines of good feng shui which advise that the building behind you should be slightly higher than yours and the buildings to the left and right should not be higher than the buildings behind. This creates the green dragon/white tiger configuration that describes classically excellent feng shui. When designing and planning your corporate head office you might want to take these rules on landscape feng shui into account. Even if you do nothing else this would strengthen your feng shui.

The building illustrated here has excellent feng shui. This is because it has a tall building behind, and two slightly taller ones to the side to give protection. It also has some empty space in front symbolizing the good 'bright hall', while the curved road to its door represents a river bringing good wealth.

Landscape Feng Shui

In front of you there should be empty land. This is a most auspicious feature, and if you are able to tap its good effect it is even better than having a view of water. If there is a patch of empty space in front of your building, then I very strongly suggest that you enlarge your main door to welcome in all that marvellous good chi (or success energy) accumulating there. Use a glass door (instead of a solid door) so that the chi can come right in! This does not mean you may not have a solid door further inside the building, but it is excellent to keep the door apparently open to capture the chi.

In Singapore there is a brand new building which faces the small empty space of a bank building, and there are three massive planters in front of its main entrance that resemble 'offerings'. This is a wonderful sign of auspicious good fortune, since it appears as if the bank is making the offerings! This is excellent for business.

Every high-rise building must have a proper main entrance and a proper back door. Buildings that have too many doors and entrances, to an extent that it is not possible to identify the main entrance, suffer from fluctuating fortunes that will finally even cause it even to collapse. Symbolically this means that the company it houses will have no sense of direction. There will be frequent changes of ownership and management.

Redeveloping is Bad For Business

I was recently in Singapore on a business trip and had tea with a new friend I had met in India. Derek is the son of a family who owned one of Singapore's small but successful banks. Unfortunately the horrible financial and economic crisis which hit South-East Asia, and especially Indonesia, in recent years has taken its toll of companies in all the countries of the region. Derek's family bank was one of those hit. I had witnessed Derek's great generosity and kind heart at first hand and felt genuinely sad at what was befalling his family. But Derek's sense of humour was wonderful as he said: 'They say if you redevelop your building and pull down your signboard your business will collapse. We redeveloped our building and had not even finished before the bank was gone!'

Respect Your Building's History

Indeed Derek was right. This is a cardinal rule of business feng shui. No matter how much

you want to take advantage of advances in the construction industry and no matter how much the land on which the original building stands has gone up in value, your head office building should be sacrosanct. Pull down the building that saw your family business flourish and, it is not going too far too say, you could well be signing the death warrant of your business.

So do resist the temptation of higher plot ratios and greater financial gains. Respect the good feng shui of the old building which brought so much wealth. Renovate it with modern façades but do not pull it down. By damaging your corporate headquarters' foundations, you will damage your entire business as well.

It is never considered good feng shui to pull down and re-develop your old office. You can renovate and refurbish the existing building, but always respect the original building which supported the business from its inception.

THE FRONT PART OF YOUR HOME

A 'Bright Hall' Brings Great Fortune

To bring good fortune to your house you need to have a big front door that opens out onto your garden, your 'bright hall'. Try to leave the door open for part of the day to encourage the chi to come in.

The 'bright hall' of feng shui is a super-important feature to try to arrange for your home. It is for this reason that whenever my friends ask my advice on buying a new home, I always advise them to select a house that faces a playing field. With empty land in front of you, there is no way you will not become prosperous. And if you are lucky enough to have a house with a good garden you must make sure that you position your door to open out into the garden. Then keep that part of the garden empty of trees and too many plants. Small low-level shrubs are fine but not plants that grow too tall.

Good Chi

In my part of town in Kuala Lumpur, Malaysia, we have a supermarket that is doing so well and making so much money, it has become the talk of the area. Apart from excel-lent service and good prices the TMC mini- market also has excellent feng shui. It has a door so wide – about 7½ metres (25 ft) and directly facing an empty piece of land (the 'bright hall'), that it appears as if the whole supermarket opens onto the bright hall. If you are greedy and really want to capture the good chi of your own 'bright hall', then make your front door big. When the door is big more of the prosperity chi will flow into your home. Then make sure the door stays open for at least a part of the day – as logically a closed door cannot admit chi into the home.

In the case of TMC, not only do they have big doors but they have also placed all their cash registers directly facing their bright hall! They will therefore continue to flourish and prosper as long as the piece of land across the road from their front door stays undeveloped.

Winding Pathways Slow Down Good Chi

Use decorative stepping stones to create a winding pathway in your garden. This provides the linkages from one part of the garden to the next. No matter how small your garden is, these pathways always slow down the energy of the dragon, that ultimate symbol of good luck, thereby making it very auspicious.

I use round concrete slabs to simulate coins, but any shape and any kind of pathway will do the job. If you want you can place a series of stepping stones resembling Chinese coins that ends in the vicinity of your main door. Your pathway can be made of pebbles, stones, wood or even tar – just make certain it is curved and not in a straight line. If you do have a straight path, and you do not want

Decorative stepping stones can be used to make a winding path that leads you through your garden to the front door. It also links one part of the garden to the next.

to make any changes, then you must make sure the straight pathway does not stop directly in front of a door. A straight pathway has the potential to become a 'poison arrow' aiming hostile energy.

How Flower Colours Enhance Your Home

It is a very good idea to have some flowering plants in your front garden. This is particularly auspicious when the front part of your garden is facing South, or South-east and South-west. You can also use any shade of red to dominate at the front of your home. These can vary from the light pinks of carnations and fuschias to the deep dark reds of peonies and roses.

Compass sector of your garden	Auspicious colours of flowers
North	Blue, purple
South	Reds and yellows – all shades
East	Blues and purples
West	White
South-east	Same as East
South-west	Same as South
North-east	Same as South
North-west	Same as West

Flowers that are any shade of red are good to plant in your front garden as red will encourage yang energy into the home.

149

Plants to Attract Precious Yang Energy

Gardens play a crucial role in enhancing your good feng shui. Having a garden around you, however small, attracts precious yang energy to surround your home. The presence of healthy green and growing plants welcomes in the vital energy that brings auspicious luck.

A home filled with vibrant growing plants immediately suggests the presence of the dragon's cosmic breath. In the old days, one method feng shui masters used to locate the auspicious dragon's lair was by looking at the lushness of greenery along hillsides. It was where grass grew strong, vibrant and lush, that represented the place where the green dragon resided. Such places as those were deemed to enjoy an abundance of the cosmic breath, the good sheng chi.

If you have 'missing corners' in your house layout, you can use plants symbolically to fill the empty space. The sketch shows a house that has a U shape, with the empty space being in the centre. Note that plants have been used to regularize the empty space.

The central part of this building is missing so plants have been used to fill the space and bring in good yang energy.

Plant Care

Healthy growing plants are always a good idea. Having said that, however, here are some feng shui guidelines concerning them.

- Try to leave the space directly in front of your main front door empty of plants. Here it is far more auspicious to try and achieve the effect of the 'bright hall' (see Tip 146).
- Trim your plants at least once every three weeks. Overgrown plants that send out branches all over the place are bad feng shui.
- Get rid of all dried leaves and faded blooms. Anything dead creates yin energy that creates negative feng shui energy.
- Be careful of plants with thorns being too near the vicinity of your front door. Such plants create protective energies that are welcome, but they should not be too near the door.
- Always make certain that the East and South-east of your garden is covered with lush greenery and blooms. Healthy plants in this part of the garden bring you wealth luck.

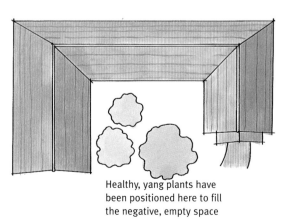

Healthy, yang plants have been positioned here to fill the negative, empty space

Beware of Bad Luck Aimed at the Door

Poison arrows are structures and features in the surrounding environment which cause bad feng shui and result in severe ill fortune and bad luck for the people whose homes are affected by them.

Effective feng shui practice requires the ability to spot the secret poison arrows of one's environment. It takes some experience to identify these harmful structures because many of them at first appear very innocent and quite harmless. So even something that is as natural as a road can be a poison arrow if it approaches your home. It is considered especially unlucky if the road comes directly towards your main front door as a long and straight road.

Right The driveway of this home is good feng shui as it is curved, and the water feature facing the front door will help to bring good fortune. The pillars could have been a problem, but they have been designed so that no poison arrows hit the front door.

Curving path and good water feature

Left The curved driveway here is good, but the tree opposite has grown too large and has become a poison arrow. It would be far better to chop it down.

Curving path but tree is poison arrow

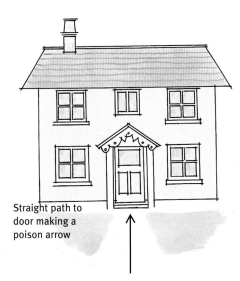

Straight path to door making a poison arrow

Left The straight path that leads up to this front door is a poison arrow. This killing energy can be severe and it is better to relocate the front door. If this is not possible an eight-side PA KUA mirror or a five rod windchime over the front door can help to alleviate the problem.

Other 'Poison Arrows'

The more obvious poison arrows that may be hitting your main door in the outside environment include:

- a straight road.
- a triangular roof line.
- a high wall nearby.
- a transmission tower.
- a telephone pole.
- A tree trunk.
- a tall straight building.
- the edge of two walls.

151

A Door Flanked By Water Spells Tears

I once visited the mansion of a very powerful and popular Minister who was also a very good friend of mine. I was immediately taken aback by the large 'moat' the Minister had surrounding the mansion. Visitors had to cross a bridge that was placed over the moat. Inside the moat were stunning Japanese carp and beautiful water lilies. Despite these lucky features, the water was wrong. I did not have the heart to tell my friend that water on both side of the front door means tears. I did not want to offer unsolicited advice. Thinking back I should have done because my poor friend has since suffered defeat in an important election, had to put up with infidelity, and suffered unfortunate and rather humiliating events.

So, in your eagerness to introduce a water feature into your home, please note these three points.

- Make sure the positioning of your water feature is correct. In all my talks, I strenuously warn against the introduction of water into your garden or home without first checking very carefully where to put it.
- Never overdo the presence of water since too much water can spell extreme bad luck, especially when also placed incorrectly. It is for this reason that I always frown on swimming-pools in private homes. They are simply too large a mass of water to take lightly. Pools are great in clubs and condominiums but can be very dangerous in private residences where the land area is too small. Such pools could well drown you.
- Do not place water on both sides of your main door. This spells tears, i.e. severe loss, a sudden fall from power and, sometimes, even death.

Water features such as this one with water lilies and fish can be beautiful but they need to be positioned carefully. Never put them on both sides of the house or on the right, the ideal place for them is on the left-hand side.

Auspicious Feng Shui Gate Design

Your gate should be at least 70 per cent solid and ideally should not have holes in it. I personally have holes in my gate as a compromise – i.e. to see who is at the gate when I receive visitors and also to allow the breeze through. But feng shui recommends solid gates.

It is also very auspicious to design a gate that has the centre higher than the sides. This symbolizes that one will attain all of one's goals. If your gate has the centre lower than the sides, it signifies failure in your career.

Gates which dip in the centre with an open pattern are not thought to be auspicious (left). The best type of gate is a solid one with a higher centre (above) as this suggests that all goals will be achieved.

Please remember that although your gate is not your main front door, it is the entrance into your home. Thus, although the direction and feng shui of your main door is more important than that of your gate, it is nevertheless advisable to make certain that your gate is not hit by secret 'poison arrows' (see Tip 150 for more on these).

Fu Dogs For Protection

For protection against every kind of bad luck, traditional Chinese homes are seldom without a pair of Fu dogs. There are no rules on what size these Fu dogs should be, but they should always balance and reflect the size of the home they are supposed to be guarding!

Fu dogs should ideally be placed high up. They can also be placed at table level but they should not be on the floor. Always put them on a stand of some kind. Fu dogs are easy to find in Chinese pottery and ceramic shops. Both Taiwan and China in recent years have been exporting exquisitely authentic copies of traditional Fu dogs.

My dogs are made of ceramic and are 60cm (2 ft) high. I place them high up on either side of my gate.

A Spacious Foyer Brings Good Feng Shui

The foyer or hallway of my home has several features with feng shui significance that are worth noting.

- There are two panels to the door. The open door is the larger of the two. This is an auspicious feature.
- Unfortunately the door faces a wall about 6 metres (20 ft) away. Ordinarily this is not good so I have placed hanging plants between the wall and the door.
- I make sure the hanging plants, mainly orchids, are flowering all the time. As soon as the flowers fade I change them. This creates good energy for the tiny 'bright hall' that I have also constructed here.
- The Thai musical Buddha is the patron of wealth and good income. The Thais believe that having him in the foyer attracts in the good chi.
- My koi pond is on the left-hand side of the door. If the pond were on the right, my husband would develop a roving eye!
- A plant covers a sharp corner edge.
- The mirror does not reflect the main door and was put there to 'extend' the wall outwards because of the 'missing corner' here.

In my house we also have two front doors – one each for me and my husband. This was necessary because we have different sheng chi directions. What is great for me is deadly for him and vice versa. We therefore enter and leave the house through different doors. Over the years I have discovered that this has benefited us enormously.

My Good Foyer

A Door panels with one open.
B Good, healthy hanging plants obscuring wall.
C Musical Buddha for encouraging good wealth and income.
D Koi pond on left-hand side of door.
E Plant covering sharp corner.
F Mirror to extend wall outwards, but not reflect front door.

Place a Family Altar Auspiciously

Many Chinese homes house a family altar and the Chinese believe that the most auspicious place to locate it is in the part of the hall that directly faces the front door so that the minute we walk into our homes we see the altar. In accordance with feng shui I also recommend that the altar be placed in the North-west part of the house or room since this direction represents heaven.

The altar should be clean at all times. Joss sticks and incense should never be allowed to appear uncared for. This is especially important if the altar is placed directly facing the front door. The deity or holy object should also always be placed in an elevated position. Keeping the altar lights turned on at all times attracts in the good chi energy. It is even more powerful than having a crystal chandelier. In my home I have activated both – altar lights and a chandelier!

If you would like to emulate the Chinese and have a family altar in your home, you need to put it in the North-west corner of your home or facing the front door. Keep it clean at all times and regularly remove any burnt incense.

Home Altar

Those of you who have them might want to take note of the following basic guidelines on the placing of family altars.

- The deity or holy object (whether statue or painting) should not share a wall with a toilet. It is most inauspicious.
- The deity or object should not be directly below a toilet upstairs. This, too, is most inauspicious.
- The deity should not be placed directly facing the door into the toilet. This direction is most inauspicious.

- The deity should not be sitting directly underneath an exposed overhead beam.
- The deity should not be directly facing a staircase. It is most inauspicious.
- The deity should not be underneath a staircase since this means that residents will regularly step over the deity. This is most inauspicious.
- The deity should not be placed in any bedroom where the resident is having sex regularly. This is very inauspicious.
- The deity should always be placed indoors or with a roof over its head.

156

Make Your Front Door Lucky

Having a water feature on the left near your front door (inside looking out) can bring good luck. Fill the pond with carp or goldfish and healthy plants. A water filter needs to be fitted so that clean water is constantly flowing and bringing in good yang energy.

In addition to protecting the front door from being hurt by the bad energy of external 'poison arrows' (see Tip 150), it is also important that the space around it be properly designed with auspicious feng shui features.

The best feature to have near the vicinity of the front door is a water feature. This can be a miniature fountain, an artificial waterfall or a fish pond like the one in the illustration. With this kind of water feature you can add fresh plants and flowers, and you can make the water flowing so that fresh yang energy is being created continuously through the day.

Build the water feature on the left side of the door (i.e on the left when you are inside looking out) and fill the pond with carp, goldfish, the arowana fish or terrapins. Do not mix fish with terrapins. Decide which you prefer and keep only one species.

It is vital that the water filter is kept turned on throughout the day and night so that the water is always clean and flowing. Feed your fish with high protein food that also contains vitamins. This makes their scales glow with good fortune.

157

Front Doors Should Not Face a Toilet

Toilets cause real havoc when they are located in the vicinity of the front door. Try to avoid having a guest toilet located directly in front of the door. If your toilet can be seen from the front door, you should try to change the toilet door, so that it is entered from another wall or, if there is sufficient space, place a solid divider (a curtain is not solid enough) to separate the toilet door from the front door.

Toilets above the main door also create extreme bad luck. The negative energy from the toilet above permeates the ceiling and flows downwards, severely afflicting the door and bringing very bad luck to residents. If you have this problem, you should try either to change the location of the toilet, or change the location of the main door. If you are planning a new bathroom you should definitely ensure that your main door is clear of any toilets upstairs.

If you have this problem and are unable to move either the door or the toilet, then the only thing you can do is to shine a very bright light upwards at the ceiling in a symbolic attempt to push the bad chi away from the main door. This can only be partially successful but it is better than nothing.

The location of your toilet is very important as it is a negative area. It needs to be screened off if it is seen from the front door.

The Taboos of the Main Door

The feng shui of the main door is the single most important feature to get right. This is the 'kou' or 'mouth' of your living space. It is through the main door that all your good luck comes to you. It is also the place where good luck can so easily be transformed into bad luck.

It is not enough only to place auspicious features near the main door. In fact, more important than that, you must watch out for all the things that should not be near the main door. I have already dealt with the taboo of toilets.

Ideally, your main door should always open into a large and spacious room – the living room is perfect for this purpose. If it opens into the dining room, the residents will think only of eating. If it opens into the kitchen all the luck of the family could get washed away. There will also be rivalry and a lot of anger in the household. If it opens too near a bedroom, where the energy is yin the people who live in the house will become indolent and lazy.

Your front door should ideally open onto a wide hall or a small foyer as detailed here. It should not face another door as the chi will just race through, so here a screen has been place to stop this happening. The staircase is to the side of the door which is good feng shui.

Further guidelines concerning the main door

● Do not let your main door open into a cramped space. If your foyer or hallway is too small, either do not have a foyer at all, or place a mirror on a wall of the foyer that does not reflect the door directly. The 'bright hall' works on both sides of the door.

● Do not let the main door open on to a long straight corridor. This is like having a poison arrow pointed at your back each day as you leave the home and aimed at your heart when you return. Place a screen like the one shown in the illustration to block the killing energy.

● The screen is also very useful when your main door is in a straight line with two other doors. This three doors in a row configuration makes the energy rush through, transforming it into killing energy. Placing a screen between the doors is a good solution to this problem.

159

Avoid Hostile Pillars Facing the Main Door

You can entice chi into your home by displaying flutes, as shown, or other small musical instruments or a print of musicians.

A square pillar similar to this faces my main door directly and its sharp edge creates an average size 'poison arrow' that attacks the good luck entering my home. To cope with this small problem, I am making use of a very beautiful and lush plant, the leaves of which effectively dissolve the hostility of the sharp edge simply by covering it.

Plants

You can use any kind of plant to camouflage any pillars or sharp corners that may be creating hostile energies for you but the leaves must be lush and green. A fake plant is also acceptable. On the wall behind, which is also visible from the door, I have hung a copy of a painting of three beauties playing the flute. This is an excellent way of enticing in the wonderful sheng chi (or success luck). As for the painting, you too can use any kind of painting, poster or print of a musician. Welcoming the luck in with music is a very ancient Asian tradition which has its original roots in feng shui.

Pillars in the home can look very attractive but if they are square the edges can give off harmful poison arrows. Work out where the arrows are hitting, and to counteract them put tall healthy plants in front of the offending edges to soften them.

Make Your Staircase Lucky and Auspicious

The staircase is often neglected by feng shui practitioners. This is such a pity because there are so many wonderful ways of enhancing the feng shui of the staircase so that you encourage good fortune to rise and make its way up and into the family's living quarters.

Always keep the staircase and the landing well lit since this attracts the chi (or good energy) to flow up the stairs.

Hang an auspicious painting on the landing. Mine has the 'fook', the Chinese word for good fortune, incorporated into it.

If your staircase is narrow, one way to overcome this is to hang a large mirror to visually widen it. This will allow greater good fortune to flow upwards.

I place a pot of peacock feathers here as further enticement for the good luck to come upstairs.

My staircase steps are completely solid. There are no holes between the steps. This ensures that any money that the family possesses does not seep out. If your staircase does has holes between the steps, you should immediately close them up with some additional pieces of wood.

Encouraging Chi

Good energy needs to be encouraged to flow positively through the home, so make sure that:

● your stairs are solid, if not fill them in.
● the stairs are well lit to encourage beneficial chi to come into the house.
● there is an inviting feature, such as an auspicious picture, or one with a good luck symbol on the landing.
● if your staircase is narrow you visibly widen it, possibly using a large mirror.

161 Double the Luck of Your Dining Room

The family dining room can be made extremely auspicious if one wall of the room is completely covered with a wall mirror. This is shown in the illustration. It shows the dining table where my small family eat together when we are not entertaining friends. The table is a small size, so each time we eat it appears that it is simply overflowing with food – excellent feng shui symbolism. The mirror then proceeds to double the wealth of food on the table.

Next, I have made the shape of this family table round. The Chinese love round dining tables because this shape represents metal, which is another word for gold or money. Round is also representative of the luck from heaven. Having said this I should add that square and rectangular tables are equally lucky.

It is also an excellent idea if the dining room has a wall or door that opens into a small courtyard. This will attract good fortune into a place where the family gathers together every day. Position auspicious flowering and fruiting plants in the courtyard. Flourishing orange or lime plants would be an ideal choice.

Here is my family's dining table. It is an auspicious round shape and the full-length mirror opposite doubles the wealth of food on the table.

Fuk Luk Sau

These are the gods of health, wealth and longevity and they are a most important addition to dining rooms. You can place them on a high side table in your dining room to ensure that your family always have something to eat and that they are healthy enough to eat the good food available. The gods can be made from ceramic or metal and can be bought from any Chinese supermarket.

The Importance of Kitchen Locations

It is useful to understand that kitchens are not places where good luck can be created. They are, however, excellent for pressing down on bad luck. So, if, for any particular year, a certain direction has bad luck, according to feng shui guidelines, then having the kitchen located there will keep the bad luck under control. Similarly if any direction represents bad luck for you according to the KUA formula (see Tip 2), then a kitchen placed there kills off your bad luck.

From a feng shui perspective the kitchen is, therefore, important as a useful method of countering bad luck in your living space.

The Oven or Cooker

Ovens or cookers should never be placed in the North-west part of the kitchen. This creates the vastly unlucky situation of having a 'fire at heaven's gate'. The outcome of this arrangement is either that your house will burn to the ground or you will suffer severe financial loss. Please try to observe this guideline as the bad luck incurred is extreme.

Also bear in mind that the cooker should not be next to the sink, the refrigerator or the washing machine since this will create a clash between the fire and water elements. This clash of elements causes quarrels and misunderstandings in the family. The situation is made worse if the cooker and the water structure or appliance are directly opposite each other in direct confrontation.

Kitchen Guidelines

● The kitchen should be in the inner half of the home.
● Never let the kitchen be too near the front door.
● As you enter the home, kitchens are better placed on the left than on the right-hand side. This keeps the white tiger under control.
● It is better not to have the back door located in the kitchen.
● Do not put mirror or mirror tiles in the kitchen. These can cause severe misfortune to befall the family.
● Kitchens should have at least one window. Windowless kitchens are both impractical as well as bad feng shui.

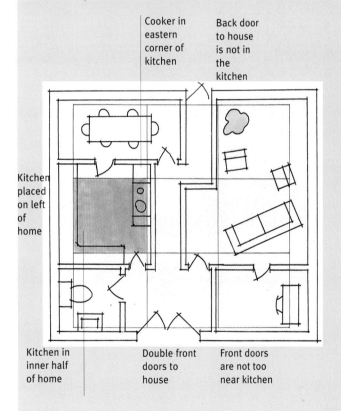

Cooker in eastern corner of kitchen

Back door to house is not in the kitchen

Kitchen placed on left of home

Kitchen in inner half of home

Double front doors to house

Front doors are not too near kitchen

163 Enhance the Flow of Chi in Your Room

Good Energy Flow

Open-plan rooms create a feeling of light and spaciousness. As you enter the room it is better to face a wall rather than windows so that the chi does not rush out. Place furniture carefully so that the chi meanders around it in a leisurely manner (left and below).

There should be at least one solid wall in any living room and this wall should preferably be directly facing the door into the room. This allows good energy or chi to flow into, and around the room, instead of escaping through windows that may have been placed directly opposite the door.

When arranging the layout of your rooms, be sensitive to the flow of traffic as you move from one room to the next. Try to allow for a meandering flow because this causes the chi to be beneficial. One way of doing this is to place connecting doors diagonal to each other.

Archways

As you can see in the illustration, my way of doing this is to have very large and wide archways connecting one room to the next.

This not only gives me a feeling of spaciousness (which is always excellent), it also enables me to use plants and furniture to create the meandering flow of energy that I want to achieve. It is not always necessary to have many walls in the home. Large archways create a better energy flow than many small rooms connected by a series of doors.

Cures For Corners and Beams

164

I have always told my friends that it is impossible to get everything correct in feng shui. In my house, for instance, I have quite a number of protruding corners and exposed overhead beams. An example of similar beams is illustrated. These imperfect feng shui structures are due to continuous additions and renovation to our house. As our incomes have improved our home has become bigger and bigger but these additions often cause unsightly structural beams to be exposed.

For the exposed beam I use a windchime to dissolve the killing energy emanating from the beam. I also make sure that the table is placed away from under the beam so that no one sits directly below it.

Disguising Corners With Plants

For protruding corners I have used a very high foliage plant, similar to the one shown, which covers the edge of the wall very effec-

Beams are not good structures in feng shui as they give off bad energy. In this kitchen windchimes should be hung to disperse this bad shar. The table is sited away from the beam which will make family meals more harmonious.

tively. In fact, every corner edge and every pillar in my home will have a plant in front of it. These plants usually last for only six months after which they usually succumb to the 'poison arrow' of the edge. They wilt and die off and have to be replaced. Hence sometimes I use some fake plants, which is quite acceptable in the practise of feng shui.

Magnify Your Luck With Secondary Doors

165

One of the most effective ways of either facing or enhancing the feng shui of your home is to have a secondary door located in the part of the house, the ruling element of which supports or produces the element of the main door (see also Tip 11). For example, if your main door is facing South and this is an auspicious direction and location for you, then having a secondary door in the East or South-east will magnify the luck of the whole house. This is because the element of the East and South-east is wood, and wood produces the fire element of the South. The elements are thus in harmony.

Harmonizing Two Doors

Main door	Secondary door
South	East and South-east
North	West and North-west
East or South-east	North
West or North-west	South-west or North-east
South-west / North-east	South

Take Care of Your Bedroom Feng Shui

It is sometimes difficult to get one's feng shui perfect in every respect. I have to place my bed under a window because I wanted to tap my best direction. Placing the bed anywhere else in the room also had me sleeping under an overhead beam. So I chose this arrangement as, on balance, it was the best feng shui solution.

I benefit from the good luck of sleeping with my head pointed to my best direction, but I suffer from the occasional attack of insomnia because of the unbalanced energy. Most of the time I keep the curtains drawn in order to close out the window. This does help to alleviate the problem of the window to some extent.

Thus, you simply cannot get everything perfect according to feng shui. No one can get their feng shui 100 per cent correct. Getting a

Bedrooms should be kept as simple as possible as they are a place of rest. Always position the bed diagonally opposite the door against a solid wall, away from a window.

Creating Restful Bedrooms

Try these tips as to enhance your bedroom's feng shui.

● Place all bedrooms in the upper part of the house.
● Do not have the doors of bedrooms directly confronting each other. This creates confrontations between all the residents.
● Do not have odd shapes for bedrooms. L- shaped rooms caused by attached bathrooms are not auspicious. Squares and rectangles are the best shapes for bedrooms.
● Do not have a bedroom that forces you to place the bed between the bedroom door and the door of an ensuite toilet.
● Place the bed diagonally opposite the door.
● Do not sleep with your head or your feet directly pointed at the bedroom door.
● The bedroom door should not directly face a staircase, a toilet, or anything sharp like the edge of opposite walls.
● Do not place the bed under an exposed beam.
● Do not place the bed under a window. Sleeping with a window directly above the bed creates unbalanced sleep and is generally not advisable.

feng shui consultant in will not help. It is better for you to understand all the options facing you, to understand the different feng shui methods and techniques you can apply, and then choose from various alternatives.

The formulae on directions and locations are excellent according to the tables in Tips 1 and 2 but if you cannot tap into them in your present room, then you will have to choose another method of enhancing your feng shui.

Too Many External Corners and Pillars

Houses and buildings that have too many corners resemble a porcupine, sending out sharp arrows. This is because there will be some sharp edges creating and shooting out 'killing energy'. Neighbours are certain to be negatively affected by these arrows, and may retaliate. In the end both you and your neighbours suffer from bad energy which consequently brings extreme bad luck.

Corners

If you have the chance to design the elevations of your home, do try to reduce the number of corners. Fewer corners and a more regular shape is better from a feng shui perspective.

Pillars

Pillars under the house on the ground floor may look visually pleasing but from a feng shui perspective, they are most inauspicious. These pillars with no walls cause all the good chi to flow right through. Nothing can be retained. The chi cannot accumulate. Businesses located in such buildings seldom survive more than about three years. The foundation is missing. The pillars need to be closed up with walls and rooms created inside them.

The Feng Shui of Pillars

Although this modern building design has pleasant curves, and not many sharp corners, the supporting pillars at the bottom are letting good chi flow right through, rather than accumulating in the building's structure. Any businesses that are located in this type of building would seldom survive more than three years as the foundation is missing. These spaces should be closed up with walls and the ground floor filled with shops or small offices.

A Proper Roof For Protective Shelter

A cardinal rule of feng shui relates to the concept of shelter. For your personal space to be auspicious, it must have proper shelter so that you are protected from the elements – the wind, the rain and the sun.

Houses with flat roofs are deemed to have inadequate shelter. It is, therefore, advisable to build a proper roof. The usual triangular shape is excellent because it allows excess water to flow down and not collect on the rooftop. This triangle, however, can cause problems to neighbours if the peak of the triangle directly points at someone's door. Try not to let this happen since, if your neighbour also practises feng shui, he or she could use a Pa Kua mirror to counter your roof, in the process sending harmful energy your way.

Blue Roof Tiles

One of the four danger indications in the I Ching has to do with the concept of 'water on top of mountain'.

According to feng shui masters, water on top of the mountain breaks its banks and spills over causing loss, hunger and death. Water on the roof is therefore considered extremely bad feng shui. Blue roof tiles symbolize water and I have seen residents of such houses suffer horrendous losses and heartbreak. I therefore strongly advise against the use of blue or black tiles. The best tiles to use for the roof are maroon-coloured or red ones.

Pyramid Roofs

In recent years this shape of roof has become popular. The pyramid shape is a mysteriously powerful one that has wonderful yin energies. It is auspicious when used for museums and other places that need yin energy. They are not suitable for yang dwellings and could well cause losses or illness. They are, therefore, unsuitable for office blocks and shopping complexes.

Roofs with triangular shapes are considered to be good to protect the home as they let negative rainwater drain away. Red or maroon roof tiles are better than blue ones which symbolize water and bad luck.

Picture Credits

The author and publishers
are grateful to the following for
permission to reproduce
photographs:

Abode: p. 13 above, 30 below, 47, 88,
149, 155; Jane Burton/Bruce Coleman:
p. 93, 144; Camera Press: p. 52, 95;
Brian Carter/Garden Picture Library: p.
142; Centennial Publishing Plc: p. 19,
25, 30 above, 31, 43, 44, 53, 56, 61,
64, 72, 98, 117, 119, 120 below, 147,
150 below, 156, 157; Christie's Images:
p. 29, 38, 48 above, 63 right, 75 below,
103, 108 above, 120 above, 126; Peter
Cooke/View: p. 100, 124-125; Liz
Eddison/Bruce Coleman: p. 18; Chris
Gascoigne/View: p. 84, 89,
90-91, 127 above & below; Jonas
Grau/Eye Ubiquitous: p. 76; Juliet
Greene/Garden Picture Library: p. 20;
Jerry Harpur: p. 23, 58 right, 81, 141
above, 145 left; Sunniva Harte/Garden
Picture Library; p. 129; Nick
Hufton/View: p. 32 below, 148 below;
Jacqui Hurst/Garden Picture Library:
p. 26 right; Ken Lucas/Planet Earth
Pictures: p. 121; Robert Maier/Bruce
Coleman: p. 21; Mayer/Le Scanff/Garden
Picture Library: p. 141 below;
Popperfoto: p. 37, 55; Powerstock/Zefa:
p. 11, 79, 123, 135, 137; Hans
Reinhard/Bruce Coleman: p. 85; Jens
Rydell/Bruce Coleman: p. 63; Fritz von
der Schulenburg/Interior Archive: p. 13
below, 15, 28, 32 above, 35, 39, 40,
51, 108 below, 111, 131 right, 154 left;
Sotheby's, London: p. 109; Tony Stone
Images: p. 17, 49, 50, 58 left, 60, 65,
74, 78, 80, 92, 97, 99, 101 below, 104,
106, 107, 112, 132, 134, 136, 139,
140, 158; Friedrich Strauss/Garden
Picture Library: p. 26 left; Telegraph
Colour Library: p. 33, 57, 73, 87
below, 102, 128, 130-131, 133; V&A
Picture Library: p. 54, 75 above;
Elizabeth Whiting Associates: p. 34, 41,
70, 86, 110, 113, 145 right, 148 above,
150 below, 151, 154 right; Andrew
Wood/Interior Archive: p 22.